REDISTRIBUTION
AND THE
WELFARE SYSTEM

Evaluative Studies

This series of studies seeks to bring about greater understanding and promote continuing review of the activities and functions of the federal government. Each study focuses on a specific program, evaluating its costs and efficiency, the extent to which it achieves its objectives, and the major alternative means— public and private—for reaching those objectives. Yale Brozen, professor of economics at the University of Chicago and an adjunct scholar of the American Enterprise Institute for Public Policy Research, is the director of the program.

REDISTRIBUTION AND THE WELFARE SYSTEM

Edgar K. Browning

American Enterprise Institute for Public Policy Research
Washington, D. C.

Edgar K. Browning is associate professor of economics at the University of Virginia.

ISBN 0-8447-3170-6

Evaluative Studies 22, July 1975

Second Printing, January 1978

Library of Congress Catalog Card No. 75-15155

Printed in the United States of America

Cover maze reproduced with permission from *Maze Craze*
© 1971 Troubadour Press, San Francisco

CONTENTS

  I   **INTRODUCTION AND SUMMARY** **1**

 II **DISTRIBUTION AND REDISTRIBUTION**
       IN THE UNITED STATES **7**
       The Distribution of Money Income: An Overview ..   8
       How Many Are Poor? 10
       Government against Poverty 14
       Redistribution to the Low-Income Population 18
       Dependency among Low-Income Families? 25
       Conclusion 26

 III **ALTERNATIVE STRATEGIES FOR REDISTRIBUTION** .. **31**
       Broad-Based Cash Transfers 32
       Categorical Cash Transfers 35
       In-Kind (Consumption) Transfers 39
       In-Kind (Human Capital) Transfers 51
       Special Tax Advantages 54
       Direct Intervention in Markets 57
       Fine Tuning the Welfare System? 59

 IV **BROAD-BASED CASH TRANSFERS** **65**
       The Negative Income Tax 65
       Demogrants 81
       Wage-Rate Subsidies 83
       Substitute or Supplement? 91

  V **THE VOLUME OF REDISTRIBUTION** **95**
       On the Cost of Redistribution 96
       Money Income and Equality 111
       The Political Process and Redistribution 117

VI **CONCLUDING REMARKS** **121**

    NOTES **123**

    TABLES

2-1 Percentage Distribution of Families by Money Income Level, Selected Years, 1947-1973 8

2-2 Percentage Income Shares for Families before Direct Taxes, Selected Years, 1947-1973 9

2-3 Poverty Lines for Nonfarm Families, by Family Size, 1973, 1966, and 1959 11

2-4 Comparison of Poverty Lines for Nonfarm Families of Four and Median Family Income, 1973, 1966, and 1959 12

2-5 Selected Characteristics of Persons below the Poverty Level, 1973, 1966, and 1959 13

2-6 Social Welfare Expenditures, Fiscal Year 1973 ... 15

2-7 Social Welfare Expenditures, Selected Years, 1947-1973 16

2-8 Social Welfare Benefits to the Lowest Quartile in the Income Distribution, Fiscal Years, 1973, 1966, and 1960 19

2-9 Federal Outlays Benefiting the Poor, Selected Fiscal Years, 1964-1975 23

2-10 Selected Labor Supply Characteristics of Families at Various Income Levels, 1973, 1963, and 1953 .. 27

3-1 Alternative Policies for the Redistribution of Income 31

3-2 Hypothetical Negative Income Tax Schedule 33

3-3 Food Stamp Benefits for a Family of Four 41

3-4 Percentage Distribution of Family Expenditures, by Income Class, 1960 47

3-5 Combined Effects of Hypothetical Food and Housing Subsidies 49

4-1 Illustration of Alternate Income Guarantees, by Family Size and Composition 76

4-2 Hypothetical Wage-Rate Subsidy Plan 84

4-3 Effects of Combining FAP with Selected Existing Tax and Transfer Programs, 1970, Family of Four 92

5-1 Outlays, Tax Rates and Net Redistribution under Two Alternative Demogrant Plans, 1970 108

5-2 Effects of Two Demogrant Plans on Percentage Distribution of Money Income, 1970 110

5-3 Family Size and Number of Earners, by Percentage Distribution of Money Income, 1973 114

FIGURES

4-1 Illustration of Alternative NIT Plans 66

4-2 Coordination of a $3,000–50 percent NIT with the Federal Income Tax 79

4-3 Hypothetical Demogrant Program Financed by a Flat Rate Tax on Income 82

5-1 Effect of Hypothetical Demogrant on Tax Structure 98

5-2 The U.S. Tax-Transfer System, 1973 105

CHAPTER I

INTRODUCTION AND SUMMARY

Just over a decade ago Congress enacted the Economic Opportunity Act making it a national goal to eliminate "the paradox of poverty in the midst of plenty." Since then there has been an unprecedented transformation in government policies until today more than half of all government expenditures are on social welfare programs. Total expenditures on social welfare by all levels of government almost tripled in the brief span of eight years, rising from $77 billion in 1965 to $215 billion in 1973. Despite this vast effort, the number of Americans officially defined as living in poverty declined by less than one-third, from 33 million in 1965 to 23 million in 1973. Further, according to Census Bureau statistics, the relative standard of living of low-income families scarcely improved at all. The lowest 20 percent of families classified by money income had 5.2 percent of total money income of all families in 1965, and that figure had risen to only 5.5 percent by 1973.

There is a paradox in these figures. How could such a massive effort to redistribute income to the poor have had such a small effect? Chapter 2 examines the impact of government tax and expenditure policies on the low-income population in an attempt to answer this question. The net transfer of income (total transfers less total taxes) to the poorest 25 percent of the population is estimated to have increased from $25 billion in 1966 to nearly $80 billion in 1973. A net transfer of $80 billion to this group, when added to before-tax income, is more than adequate to have moved every family above its respective poverty line. Yet statistically 23 million remained poor.

The primary reason for this anomaly is that a large share of government transfers is simply not counted as income. Benefits from in-kind programs that subsidize the consumption of particular goods and services—such as food stamps, public housing, medicare, medicaid, and manpower training—do not remove a single person from poverty because the official poverty lines are stated in terms of *money* income. Poverty, as officially defined, is diminished when the government gives a poor person $100 in cash which is then used to purchase housing, food, and medical care, but it is not diminished when $100 worth of these goods is given outright. Yet it is clear that in-kind transfers should be counted as income since they augment the *real* incomes of recipients almost as effectively as cash transfers.

According to data from the Department of Health, Education and Welfare, federal in-kind transfers to those still officially poor after receiving cash transfers in 1973 were more than half of all transfers received. When in-kind transfers are counted as income, the average income of those officially counted as poor in 1973 was 30 percent *above* their average poverty line. Therefore, in a meaningful sense poverty had become virtually nonexistent in America by 1973. The vast increase in government expenditures over the past decade has effectively redistributed income to the low-income population. It only remains to recognize that government statistics on the money incomes of low-income families are totally unreliable as a measure of the real incomes of these families.

More than one hundred separate programs combine to form the welfare system that accomplishes this enormous redistribution. Since it would be impossible to discuss each program in detail, and since most of them fall into a few general categories, the approach taken in Chapter 3 is to examine these general categories. We begin with a brief discussion of the negative income tax (NIT), the policy favored by many economists, and then use the NIT as a benchmark against which to evaluate alternative policies.

The negative income tax is a simple cash transfer program structured so that the lower the pretransfer income of a family, the larger the amount of the transfer. The major criticism of this policy has been that it may weaken work incentives, since a family loses part of the transfer if it earns more on its own. The analysis in Chapter 3 suggests, however, that other policies have defects much greater than the NIT. In fact, *most existing programs are simply very poor copies of the NIT, sharing all of its defects and adding several more.* For instance, Aid to Families with Dependent Children and Supplemental Security Income are nothing more than NIT plans restricted to certain demographic groups. The food stamp program is an NIT containing the requirement that recipients must spend a large part of their net income on food. Thus, the United States already has several modified NIT plans in existence, but each of them causes severe distortions in the allocation of resources and produces inequities that could be avoided through the use of an outright NIT. In sum, the analysis supports the views of those who hold that a well-designed NIT is preferable to alternative methods of redistributing income.

As unsatisfactory as these individual welfare programs appear to be, their combined effects are generally much worse. Because many low-income families receive transfers from several programs, it is essential that these programs be well coordinated. They are not. Not only do major inequities exist, but also the combined impact of several programs on work incentives is often disastrous. At a minimum, poor families are subjected to effective tax rates on earnings of 40 to 45 percent, which is approximately the effective tax rate on earnings for a family receiving only food stamps. For families that also receive benefits under other programs, tax rates are generally much higher, ranging up to 80 percent and even exceeding 100 percent in some cases. This difficulty, the "cumulative tax rate" problem resulting from piling one program atop another, is but one indication of the difficulty of coordinating several major programs with overlapping coverage. The current welfare system is so complex that problems of this type abound, and are probably the unavoidable outcome of attempting to "fine tune" the system with scores of programs rather than relying on a few simple ones that could be understood and coordinated effectively.

Since the analysis of Chapter 3 suggests that the NIT is an attractive alternative to existing programs, Chapter 4 examines this policy in greater detail. Predictably, it is concluded that the NIT is no panacea and that a number of hard choices would have to be made in designing any specific NIT program. Where should the policy variables be set? How should income be defined? How should families of different sizes be treated? And what provision should be made for hardship cases? Unhappy compromises are required, but this is true of all redistributive policies, not just the NIT. And the NIT has the advantage of making it easier to understand the issues involved.

Chapter 4 also analyzes a proposal that has attracted some attention in recent years: the wage-rate subsidy. Supplementing wage rates rather than incomes can overcome one of the major defects of the NIT, its impact on work incentives. Under a wage-rate subsidy, the transfer received increases if the recipient works more, so its effect on work effort should be more favorable than that of the NIT. However, wage-rate subsidies have several defects of their own—the difficulty of concentrating the transfers on poor families, severe administrative problems, the need for a companion program to deal with those unable to work, and the difficulty of coordinating the companion program with the wage-rate subsidy. On balance, it is not clear that the work incentive advantage outweighs these other disadvantages.

Both plans could be used as either a substitute or a replacement for existing programs. However, either plan would be disastrous if it were simply added to the present system. *If an NIT were piled on top of existing programs, it would probably completely destroy the incentive of low-income families to work,* because the NIT's implicit tax rate would raise the effective tax rates on the earnings of low-income families even higher than they are now. A wage-rate subsidy would not have this effect, but it would eliminate most of the advantage to a worker from seeking out the best paying job available. This would seriously impair the ability of labor markets to allocate workers among jobs efficiently. Therefore, although the NIT and the wage-rate subsidy are attractive compared to present programs, they must be considered as alternatives. Neither can be piled on top of existing policies if its advantages are to be realized.

Without doubt, the most difficult issue in designing a welfare system is the determination of how much redistribution to carry out. The final chapter focuses on this issue. Two points are emphasized. First, it is much more difficult to finance a redistribution of income than is generally understood. For example, an NIT with an income guarantee of $5,500 for a family of four—like that proposed by the National Welfare Rights Organization in 1970—would redistribute about $71 billion, or about 8 percent of net national product, but would require marginal tax rates of at least 83 percent on *all* families in the United States. That level of taxation would obviously produce economic ruin. In general, for every 1 percent of net national product that is redistributed, marginal tax rates for all families must be raised by about five percentage points. Basically, this is because only a small part of net national product is available as a tax base to finance redistributive programs.

The second point stressed in Chapter 5 is that a large part of any additional redistribution (above that already being carried out) would not accrue to low-income families. This conclusion is based on the assumption that effective marginal tax rates on low-income families are already as high as they can safely be. In order to redistribute additional resources while avoiding higher tax rates on the poor, it would be necessary to extend transfers well up into the middle-income classes. Roughly speaking, to redistribute an additional 1 percent of net national product to the lowest 20 percent of the income distribution would probably require a redistribution of at least 1 percent more to families above that level. In other words, 2 percent of net national product would have to be redistributed to concentrate half that sum on low-income families, and this would require an increase in the marginal tax rates of all families of approximately ten percentage points. If tax rates are not allowed to rise for low-income families, they would have to rise by more than ten percentage points for other families.

These points suggest that the costs of transferring additional resources to low-income families have become quite high. This is a direct result of the explosion in social welfare spending that has taken place over the past decade. Each additional billion dollars redistributed becomes more difficult to finance, and a smaller part of each additional billion can feasibly be transferred to the poor. At the present time, with a net redistribution of about $80 billion, it seems reasonable to suggest that *efforts to improve the welfare system should now be directed to structural reform rather than to increasing the volume of redistribution.* This would not imply disregard for the welfare of the poor since a well-designed replacement for the present system would improve their well-being substantially without imposing still greater costs on taxpayers. Reform is urgent today not because of inadequate benefit levels, but because of the inequities, high administrative costs, and distortions that characterize the present system.

CHAPTER II

DISTRIBUTION AND REDISTRIBUTION IN THE UNITED STATES

Few subjects are more emotionally charged than how public policy should be used to influence the distribution of income. At issue is the question of how the total income of the society is to be divided among its citizens. It is understandable that people would have strong convictions about policies which influence their own, as well as everyone else's, incomes. A knowledge of the facts concerning the distribution of income in the United States and how government policy affects that distribution is essential if our convictions are to have a solid foundation. Unfortunately, most of us know very little about these matters: it is rare to find a person who even knows where his own income places him in the overall income scale. This chapter seeks to outline what is known about the distribution of income in America and how government affects it.

Our primary concern will be with the low-income population. Just over a decade ago Congress passed the Economic Opportunity Act which set as a national goal the elimination of "the paradox of poverty in the midst of plenty." Since then dozens of government programs have been launched in an attempt to realize that goal. Today there are more than a hundred federal government programs conferring benefits to the poor. Total social welfare expenditures increased from $77.2 billion in 1965 to $215 billion in 1973, or by about 180 percent. Despite this vast effort, the number of people officially defined as poor fell by less than a third, from 33.2 million to 23 million.[1] Indeed, many economists claim that the relative standard of living of low-income families has not improved at all.[2] A major purpose of our analysis will be to explain how such massive expenditures could have so little apparent effect.

The Distribution of Money Income: An Overview

Table 2-1 shows the percentage distribution of annual before-tax money income among families for selected years.[3] Looking at 1973, the most recent year for which data are available, we can see the apparent variation that characterizes the distribution of money income in the United States. While more than half of all families had incomes between $10,000 and $25,000, 5.9 percent were getting by on incomes reported to be less than $3,000. The lowest 5.9 percent of families had incomes that were a little less than a fourth of the median family income of $12,073. At the other end of the distribution, 9.3 percent of families had incomes above $25,000. The average before-tax income of the top 6 percent, about $37,000, was seventeen times the average income of the bottom 6 percent.

The definition of money income used by the U.S. Bureau of the Census includes such familiar components as wage and salary income, income from self-employment, and dividends and interest. It also includes many government cash-transfer payments: social security, unemployment compensation, public assistance, and others.[4] So the figures in Table 2-1 already include a substantial amount of redistribution. Thus, 5.9 percent of all families had incomes below $3,000 even after receipt of cash transfers from federal, state, and local governments.[5]

Table 2-1

PERCENTAGE DISTRIBUTION OF FAMILIES BY MONEY INCOME LEVEL, SELECTED YEARS, 1947–1973

Income Class	1973	1966	1960	1947
Under $3,000	5.9	14.3	21.6	48.9
$3,000 to $5,999	13.2	22.3	33.2	39.3
$6,000 to $9,999	19.7	33.7	30.9	9.0
$10,000 to $14,999	25.6	20.4	10.6	
$15,000 to $24,999	26.2	7.5	2.8	2.8
Over $25,000	9.3	1.7	0.9	
Median income (dollars)	12,073	7,447	5,631	3,048
Median income (constant 1973 dollars)	12,073	10,269	8,436	6,032

Source: U.S. Bureau of the Census, "Money Income in 1973 of Families and Persons in the United States," *Current Population Reports*, series P-60, no. 97 (1975), Table 21, p. 60.

Although it is clear that a sizeable number of families had low incomes in 1973, the number was dramatically smaller than in earlier years. In 1947, 48.9 percent, nearly half of all families, had incomes below $3,000, compared with only 5.9 percent in 1973. And in 1947, only 2.8 percent had incomes above $10,000, whereas more than half of all families were in that category in 1973. Over that twenty-six-year period, there was a major decrease in the percentage of families with incomes below $3,000 and an equally impressive increase in the percentage with incomes above $10,000.

Two factors are primarily responsible for these changes. The first is inflation. Prices rose by 99 percent between 1947 and 1973, so that a $3,000 income in 1973 would buy only as much as a $1,500 income bought in 1947. However, about 20 percent of families in 1947 had incomes below $1,500 (equivalent to $3,000 in 1973 prices), and this proportion had been cut by more than two-thirds by 1973. It is clear that there were sizeable gains in real income over the period—for the poor as well as others.

The second important factor is economic growth. When national income rises faster than population, individual incomes also rise, since national income is simply the sum of individual incomes. Median family income in constant 1973 dollars rose from $6,032 to $12,073 over the twenty-six-year period. This gain in real income was shared throughout the income distribution. Economic growth is primarily responsible for the reduction in the percentage of families with incomes below $3,000 (in 1973 dollars) from 20 percent to 5.9 percent.[6] It is easy to see why many economists emphasize the contribution of economic growth to a war on poverty: the poor as well as the rich share in economic growth.

A somewhat different perspective on how the distribution of income has changed is afforded by Table 2-2. This table groups

Table 2-2
PERCENTAGE INCOME SHARES FOR FAMILIES BEFORE DIRECT TAXES, SELECTED YEARS, 1947–1973

Income Group	1973	1966	1960	1947
Lowest quintile	5.5	5.6	4.8	5.1
Second quintile	11.9	12.4	12.2	11.8
Third quintile	17.5	17.8	17.8	16.7
Fourth quintile	24.0	23.8	24.0	23.2
Highest quintile	41.1	40.5	41.3	43.3

Source: U.S. Bureau of the Census, "Money Income in 1973 of Families and Persons in the United States," *Current Population Reports*, series P-60, no. 97 (1975), Table 22.

families according to whether they are in the lowest 20 percent of the income distribution, the second 20 percent, and so on. For 1973, the lowest fifth, or lowest quintile, had a combined money income of 5.5 percent of the total money income of the entire population. Perhaps the easiest way to visualize this is to say that the average money income of the lowest quintile was 27.5 percent of average income of all families. If a quintile has a share of 20 percent, this means that families in that quintile have an average income equal to the average of all families. For the lowest quintile, a share of 5.5 percent means 5.5/20, or 27.5 percent of average income. The top fifth of families had an average income of slightly more than twice the average of all families, or 41.1/20 to be exact. And the average income of the top fifth of families is 7.5 times (41.1/5.5) the average income of the bottom fifth of families.

According to Table 2-2, there have been only slight changes in the pretax income shares of each quintile since 1947. The share going to the top fifth dropped from 43.3 to 41.1 percent, and the shares of every other quintile increased slightly. Note in particular that the share of the lowest fifth increased from 5.1 percent to 5.5 percent, an improvement of only 8 percent. It is this fact that has led many people to conclude that there has been no significant *relative* improvement in the position of low-income families. And recall that these figures include cash transfer payments from government.

Even though economic growth increased the absolute incomes of families in all quintiles, the increases were in about the same proportion, leaving the relative distribution virtually unchanged. How one views the standard of living of low-income families depends to a large extent on whether one is concerned about poverty in an absolute or a relative sense. In an absolute sense, the average real money income of the lowest quintile doubled between 1947 and 1973; but so did the incomes of families in the other quintiles. Thus the comparative position of the lowest fifth of families apparently improved very little.

How Many Are Poor?

In 1965 Mollie Orshansky of the Social Security Administration formulated definitions of poverty level incomes that have been the basis for the official government definitions ever since.[7] Originally, the poverty lines were calculated by determining the cost of a "minimally adequate diet" and multiplying by three. Several adjustments have been made since 1965, the most important of which involved adjusting the poverty lines upwards as prices increased. Table 2-3 gives the poverty level incomes for nonfarm families of various sizes in 1973, 1966, and 1959. Any family with a pretax money income below the relevant poverty line is offically poor.

It is true that the official poverty lines are arbitrary. A "minimally adequate diet" is not an objective criterion. There is no obvious reason why the cost of an assumed minimum diet should be multiplied by three in order to define a poverty level income.[8] Nor does it seem appropriate to group together all families below a critical level, making no distinction between a family of four with an income of $1,000 and one with an income of $4,539. Both are considered poor, whereas a family of four with an income of $4,541 is not poor. But all definitions are arbitrary to a degree, and it would serve no useful purpose to quibble over exactly where to draw the line separating the poor from the nonpoor. It is more important that the definition be consistently applied over time. In addition, over the years so much information has been generated on the basis of this definition that we have no choice but to rely on it. However, one point should be made: the poverty lines do not represent minimum subsistence incomes. That should be clear from the fact that millions of Americans have gotten by on incomes well below the poverty lines applicable to them. Indeed, probably two-

Table 2-3

POVERTY LINES FOR NONFARM FAMILIES,
BY FAMILY SIZE, 1973, 1966, AND 1959

Family Size	Money Income		
	1973	1966	1959
1	$2,247	$1,628	$1,467
2	2,895	2,107	1,894
3	3,548	2,588	2,324
4	4,540	3,317	2,973
5	5,358	3,908	3,506
6	6,028	4,388	3,944
7 and over	7,435	5,395	4,849

Source: 1973: U.S. Bureau of the Census, *Current Population Reports*, series P-60, no. 98 (1975), "Characteristics of the Low-Income Population: 1973," Table A-3; 1966: U.S. Bureau of the Census, unpublished data; and 1959: U.S. Bureau of the Census, *Current Population Reports, Special Studies*, series P-23, no. 28, "Revision in Poverty Statistics, 1959-68," Table C.

thirds of the population of the remainder of the world have incomes below the levels which define poverty in the United States.[9]

Poverty statistics based on such a definition can be a very misleading guide for policy. Suppose, for example, that our goal is to remove as many people as possible from poverty. If the resources available to accomplish this goal are limited, the efficient policy would be to concentrate funds on those slightly below the poverty line and give nothing to the poorest families. This would remove the greatest number of families from poverty per dollar expended. Clearly this is exactly the opposite of the approach that is desirable. On the other hand, if funds are concentrated on the poorest families, the limited resources might be insufficient to move a single family above its poverty line. This policy, even though it would produce no decline in the number of families counted as poor, is clearly the preferable alternative. The important point to remember is that poverty is not an all-or-nothing matter: there are various degrees of poverty. No approach which simply counts those who are above and those who are below an arbitrary line can serve as an adequate basis for formulating policy.

The definition of poverty used by the U.S. government is an absolute definition. The poverty level of income is adjusted upward over time to account for rising prices (see Table 2-4), but that is all. Thus, a family with an income of $4,540 in 1973 could purchase only the same basket of goods as a family with $2,973 in 1959. This is the essence of an absolute definition, using a fixed real income as the measuring rod. In an economy with rising real incomes, the

---

Table 2-4

COMPARISON OF POVERTY LINES FOR NONFARM FAMILIES OF FOUR AND MEDIAN FAMILY INCOME, 1973, 1966, AND 1959

Year	Poverty Line[a]	Median Family Income[a]	Poverty Line as % of Median Family Income
1973	$4,540	$12,073	38
1966	3,317	7,447	45
1959	2,973	5,428	55

[a] Before direct taxes.

Source: U.S. Bureau of the Census, *Current Population Reports,* series P-60, no. 98, "Characteristics of the Low-Income Population: 1973" (1975), Table A-1; and U.S. Bureau of the Census, *Current Population Reports,* series P-60, no. 97, "Money Income in 1973 of Families and Persons in the United States" (1975), Table 21.

poverty line becomes a smaller percentage of median family income over time. In 1959 a family with an income equal to 50 percent of the median would have been defined as poor, but in 1972, 50 percent of median family income was well above the poverty line. Real median family income rose steadily during this period, but the poverty line remained fixed in real terms.

Table 2-5 gives some information about families with incomes below the poverty line. The total number of poor persons declined from 39.5 million in 1959 to 23.0 million in 1973, but note that most of this decline occurred before 1966. The year 1966 is an important date since it marks the approximate beginning of an acceleration in the growth of government social welfare expenditures. Social welfare expenditures increased by $38.2 billion in the seven years between 1959 and 1966, and by $127.2 billion in the following seven years.[10] The number of poor persons declined by 11 million in the first seven-year period, but only by 5.5 million in the second. However, before we conclude that the increase in spending was ineffective, our earlier warning about how misleading it is to consider only the poor versus nonpoor distinction should be recalled.

It is also useful to make distinctions among several demographic groups within the poverty population. Table 2-5 breaks down the total number of poor persons according to whether they were over sixty-five years old and whether, for those under sixty-five, the family head was male or female. The number of poor persons over sixty-five declined from 5.7 million in 1959 to 3.4 million in 1973,

Table 2-5

SELECTED CHARACTERISTICS OF PERSONS BELOW THE POVERTY LEVEL, 1973, 1966, AND 1959

(in thousands)

	1973	1966	1959
Number of poor persons	22,973	28,510	39,490
65 years and over	3,354	5,111	5,679
Under 65 years[a]			
Family with female head	9,460	7,841	8,115
Family with male head	10,160	15,558	25,695
Decrease in total number of poor from prior period	5,537	10,980	—

[a] Includes single person households.

Source: U.S. Bureau of the Census, "Characteristics of the Low-Income Population: 1973," *Current Population Reports*, series P-60, no. 98 (1975), Table 1.

whereas the number of poor persons in female-headed families increased from 8.1 million to 9.5 million. The major reduction in the poverty population was among families headed by non-aged males.

That the major reduction in the incidence of poverty occurred largely in families with non-aged male heads is a very significant fact. It is significant because this is the one category that, over the entire 1959–1973 period, had no special cash assistance program except for unemployment insurance (which is only temporarily available and was not of significant size). Government cash assistance programs, then, had little to do with the impressive reduction in poverty in this category. The decline was caused by economic growth and the higher wage rates and earnings that accompanied it. By contrast, several cash assistance programs were available for the elderly and female-headed families, but these two groups taken together experienced only a slight decline in poverty.

These figures may be misleading for several reasons. First, even though almost the same number of persons in aged and female-headed families was poor, these persons may have been less poor in 1973. In fact, this is almost certainly the case, as we will see later. Second, it is not clear exactly how many persons in each category would have been poor in the absence of government transfer programs. According to one recent estimate for 1971, 20.9 percent of all families would have been poor in the absence of government transfer programs, but that figure was reduced to 12 percent as a result of the transfers.[11] In other words, almost 9 percent of all U.S. families were made nonpoor by government transfer payments. Table 2-5, of course, includes only those who remained poor even after receipt of government assistance.

Government against Poverty

Governments affect the distribution of income in many ways, probably most importantly through the use of expenditure policies. The Social Security Administration provides aggregate data on a number of different expenditure programs in the social welfare area, and these programs are the important ones for us to consider. Table 2-6 gives social welfare expenditures by major functional category for fiscal year 1973. An impressive sum, $215.2 billion, was spent by federal, state, and local governments in that year, with the federal contribution amounting to 57 percent of the total. This comes to an expenditure of over $1,000 per person in the United States, or more than $4,000 per family of four.

Table 2-6

SOCIAL WELFARE EXPENDITURES, FISCAL YEAR 1973

($ billions)

Category	Total Expenditures	Expenditures from Federal Funds[a]	Expenditures from State and Local Funds[b]
Social Insurance	$85.9	$ 72.2	$13.7
Public Aid	28.3	17.8	10.5
Health and Medical	14.6	7.2	7.4
Veterans' Programs	13.0	12.9	0.1
Education	65.2	6.9	58.3
Housing and Other Social Welfare	8.2	5.2	3.0
Total	215.2	122.3	92.9

a Includes federal grants to state and local governments.

b Excludes federal grants to state and local governments.

Source: A. M. Skolnik and S. R. Dales, "Social Welfare Expenditures," *Social Security Bulletin*, vol. 37, no. 1 (Washington, D. C.: U.S. Government Printing Office, January 1974), Table 1.

An examination of how this $215.2 billion was allocated among the six categories—which cover over 100 separate federal programs—is informative. For the federal government, the most important category was social insurance, with 60 percent of expenditures falling under that heading. The largest programs in this category are social security (OASDI), medicare, and unemployment insurance. For state and local governments, the largest category, claiming about two-thirds of their total social welfare expenditures, was education. This category includes the construction and operation of primary and secondary schools as well as colleges and universities.

There are many programs included in social welfare expenditures which most people do not think of as welfare programs. Public schools and social security are obvious examples. Nonetheless, such programs should not be ignored in a discussion of how government affects people with low incomes. Public schools and social security payments benefit many nonpoor families, but they also benefit many poor families. The availability of public schools for the children of the poor is, in fact, of great importance to their well-being. To understand this, just imagine the burden it would be if the poor had to finance the costs of educating their children. With costs per pupil exceeding $1,000 in many areas, it is obvious that families with incomes of $4,000 or less would be unable to afford a good education for their children. Even though public schools do not fit the stereo-type of a welfare program, they must be considered in any comprehensive evaluation of the effects of government on the welfare of the poor.

It is easy to think of expenditure programs as being the only government policies that have much of an impact on the poor. However, there are other policies that should not be forgotten. For example, the poor pay taxes and this tends to reduce their incomes. In fact, governments probably collect about 20 percent to 25 percent of the incomes of the poor as tax revenue.[12] In addition to taxes, there are a number of government programs that can have a major impact on incomes without involving any significant expenditure. Minimum wage laws and regulations requiring "equal pay for equal work" are of this type. Very little is known about the distributional impact of these latter policies, so our analysis will largely be restricted to tax and expenditure policies.

Table 2-7 gives an idea of how social welfare expenditures have grown in recent years. In the twenty-six-year period from 1947 to

Table 2-7

SOCIAL WELFARE EXPENDITURES, SELECTED YEARS, 1947–1973

($ in billions, fiscal years)

	1973	1966	1959	1947
Total social welfare	$215.2	88.0	49.8	17.3
From federal funds	$122.3	45.6	23.5	9.8
From state and local funds	$ 92.9	42.4	26.3	7.5
Total social welfare as % of NNP	19.3	13.5	11.3	8.3
Total government spending as % of NNP	34.8	31.3	31.0	20.4
Total social welfare as % of total government spending	55.3	42.9	36.3	40.8
Federal social welfare as % of federal spending	49.6	33.8	25.9	26.6

Sources: A. M. Skolnik and S. R. Dales, "Social Welfare Expenditures," *Social Security Bulletin*, vol. 37, no. 1 (Washington, D. C.: U.S. Government Printing Office, January 1974), Table 1; I. C. Merriam and A. M. Skolnik, *Social Welfare Expenditures Under Public Programs in the United States, 1929-66*, U.S. Department of Health, Education and Welfare, Social Security Administration, Research Report No. 25 (Washington, D. C.: U.S. Government Printing Office, 1968), Table 1; United States Department of Commerce, Social and Economic Statistics Administration, *Survey of Current Business* (Washington, D. C.: U.S. Government Printing Office, July of appropriate year).

1973, social welfare expenditures grew from $17.3 billion to $215.2 billion. Inflation is only partly responsible for this growth: 1947 expenditures stated in constant 1973 dollars were $32.8 billion, so in real terms social welfare expenditures grew by a factor of almost seven in the twenty-six years. It is also interesting to note that state and local expenditures (mainly education) increased more rapidly up until 1966, at which time federal expenditures were only slightly above the state and local share. By 1973 federal spending exceeded state and local spending by almost a third. Note in particular the rapid growth in social welfare expenditures since 1966, especially for the federal government. In constant 1973 dollars, federal spending rose by 74 percent between 1959 and 1966, but then increased by 110 percent between 1966 and 1973.

Table 2-7 also shows what these sums mean relative to other expenditure figures. Total social welfare expenditures rose from 8.3 percent of net national product (NNP) in 1947 to 19.3 percent in 1973. It took nineteen years (from 1947 to 1966) for this percentage to rise by 5.2 percentage points (from 8.3 to 13.5), but in the following seven years the percentage rose by 5.8 points.

This massive increase in social welfare spending reflects two basic changes in government budgets. First, government spending has become increasingly important relative to net national product. Total government expenditures were only 20.4 percent of NNP in 1947 but rose to 34.8 percent by 1973. A second basic change is that a larger part of the growing government budgets—federal, state, and local—is being devoted to social welfare spending. This is particularly true for the federal government. Only 26.6 percent of total federal spending was devoted to the social welfare category in 1947, compared to almost one-half in 1973.

Spending an increasing proportion of the federal budget on social welfare means spending a reduced proportion in other areas. A number of programs have lost ground, most prominently national defense. Defense expenditures, which were 42 percent of the federal budget in 1966, had fallen to 30.8 percent in 1973. In real terms, defense spending rose by only 4 percent over this period, while federal social welfare spending rose by 110 percent. That change in the relative importance of defense and social welfare was, of course, what was meant by the phrase "reordering national priorities" that was fashionable in the late 1960s. As of 1973 it is clear that this is exactly what happened, and to an unprecedented degree in so brief a period.

It is no exaggeration to say that government spending programs have been transformed over the past decade. The most important question remaining is whether this transformation has benefited the American people, especially the low-income population in whose name it took place. In the last section we saw that, according to official statistics, the rate of decline in the number of Americans living in poverty started to slow down about the same time the explosion in social welfare spending began. Even more interesting is the fact that the share of total money income going to the lowest 20 percent of families has not changed significantly since 1947, and it has even declined slightly since 1966. Do these figures accurately reflect the consequences of the mounting social welfare expenditures? It is this question that will primarily concern us for the remainder of this chapter.

Redistribution to the Low-Income Population

It might be thought that it would be easy to determine what share of total social welfare expenditures goes to the low-income population. Such is not the case. No body of statistics directly measures the benefits received by low-income families. The reason for this is the multiplicity of separate programs involved. More than a hundred federal programs, administered by a dozen different agencies, benefit the poor; and there are many more programs at the state and local level. Different eligibility rules govern these programs. In many cases benefits are not related to family income in any easily discernible fashion. While there are a few studies that attempt to estimate the benefits by income class for specific programs, all programs are not considered simultaneously, and often the data in the studies refer to different years. Nonetheless, it is clearly important at least to attempt to consider all programs if a comprehensive measure of the volume of redistribution is to be obtained.

The approach adopted here will, of necessity, be inexact. It is based on a procedure used in earlier studies by Benjamin Okner [13] and Robert Lampman.[14] Basically, it assumes that a specific percentage of each of the categories of total social welfare expenditures (the categories listed in Table 2-6) reaches the lowest 25 percent of the population classified by income. The percentages used are given in a footnote to Table 2-8 and are those developed by Okner. These figures are the basic building blocks for the analysis. If they are incorrect, then our final estimates (in the first part of this section, at least) will be inaccurate. While the percentages used are admittedly rough estimates, my knowledge of the individual programs covered suggests that they are fairly close to the mark.

Table 2-8

SOCIAL WELFARE BENEFITS TO THE LOWEST QUARTILE IN THE INCOME DISTRIBUTION, FISCAL YEARS, 1973, 1966, AND 1960

	Fiscal Years		
	1973	1966	1960
Total social welfare ($ billions)[a]	214.6	87.6	51.4
Percentage transferred to lowest quartile[b]	47%	43%	44%
Gross transfer ($ billions)	100.7	37.6	22.8
Taxes paid ($ billions)	22.5	12.5	8.4
Net transfer ($ billions)	78.2	25.1	14.4
Education ($ billions)	11.8	5.9	3.2
Net transfer excluding education ($ billions)	66.4	19.2	11.2
Net transfer (excluding education) per capita (dollars)	1,248	387	247
Net income (excluding education) per capita (dollars)	1,812	845	603
Net transfer (excluding education) as a percentage of net income	69%	46%	41%

a Excludes expenditures within foreign countries, so the figures are slightly lower than in Table 2-7.

b A weighted average assuming that the following percentages of expenditures within each category benefit the lowest quartile:

Social insurance	54%
Public aid	87%
Health and medical	50%
Veterans	50%
Education	18%
Housing and other	50%.

Sources: A. M. Skolnik and S. R. Dales, "Social Welfare Expenditures," *Social Security Bulletin,* vol. 37, no. 1 (Washington, D. C.: U.S. Government Printing Office, January 1974), Table 1; I. C. Merriam and A. M. Skolnik, "Social Welfare Expenditures Under Public Programs in the United States, 1929-66," Department of Health, Education and Welfare, Social Security Administration, Research Report No. 25 (Washington, D. C.: U.S. Government Printing Office, March 1968), Table 1; Benjamin A. Okner, "Transfer Payments: Their Distribution and Role in Reducing Poverty," in *Redistribution to the Rich and Poor,* Kenneth E. Boulding and Martin Pfaff, eds. (Belmont, California: Wadsworth Publishing Company, 1972), pp. 62-76.

In Table 2-8, total social welfare expenditures for three recent years [15] are multiplied by a weighted average of the percentages appropriate to the separate categories of social welfare expenditures. The result, given in the third row, is the gross transfer made to the lowest quarter of the income distribution. Since taxes are paid by low-income families, it is necessary to subtract taxes from the gross transfer to arrive at the net transfer. Based on other studies, I have assumed that the lowest quartile pays 6 percent of all federal, state, and local taxes.[16] The total tax burden is shown in the fourth row. The next row gives the net transfer, the excess of transfers over taxes. The net transfer was an impressive $78.2 billion in 1973, according to Okner's method of calculation.

Note the growth in size of the net transfer. After increasing by 74 percent between 1960 and 1966, it more than tripled between 1966 and 1973. The $78.2 billion net transfer in 1973 comes, of course, from the upper three-fourths of the income distribution. (However, not all families in the upper three-fourths bore net costs, since it is probable that net transfers were also made to some families above the lowest quartile.) This represents an average cost of about $500 per capita to the upper three-fourths, or about $2,000 per family of four. Even this, however, understates the contribution made to the well-being of those in the lowest quartile. The upper three quartiles not only provided a net transfer of $78.2 billion to the lowest quartile, but they also bore the entire net cost of financing other (non-social welfare) government expenditures of $193 billion. Other government expenditures for such things as defense, police, and highways also confer benefits to those in the lowest quartile, but no attempt has been made here to estimate those benefits.

Now let us look more closely at 1973 to try to determine how over 40 percent of the bottom quartile could remain officially poor even after receipt of this enormous net transfer. First, we subtract estimated education benefits.[17] The reason for doing this, as is pointed out below, is that the benefits from public education were probably taken into account when the official poverty lines were formulated in the early 1960s. This leaves a net transfer exclusive of education of $66.4 billion. Dividing by the number of persons in the lowest quartile yields a net transfer per capita of $1,248. To this, however, must be added pretransfer income (mainly earnings), which I estimate at $564 per capita.[18] Thus, the average net income per capita was $1,812.

A per capita income of $1,812 means an average income of $7,248 per family of four. In 1973 the poverty line for a family of four was only $4,540. How could nearly half of this group still have been poor after receipt of transfers? In view of these figures it appears incredible that there was a single poor person left in the United States in 1973.

There are a number of factors which contribute to the apparent discrepancy between these figures and the existence of 23 million poor persons (43 percent of the bottom quartile) in 1973. I will begin with several that are relatively unimportant. First, the estimate of the gross transfer to the lowest quartile might be far off. I do not believe this is so, and I will present evidence a bit later that supports my estimate.

A second factor is the possibility that the distribution of transfers is so uneven that many poor families do not receive enough to raise them to their poverty lines, while others receive much more than enough. One family might receive a $10,000 transfer and another only $2,000. This might be the case to some extent, since transfers are not related to income in any direct fashion. However, transfers are not distributed unevenly enough to account for the existence of 23 million poor persons.

A third possibility relates to the differences in poverty levels for families of different size. The poverty line for an unrelated individual was $2,247, so if the bottom quartile were composed only of unrelated individuals, the net income per capita would be $1,812— a figure well below the poverty line. However, less than one-fifth of the population of the bottom quartile is composed of unrelated individuals; the rest are in families averaging three persons.[19] This reason, while contributing to the discrepancy, is only of minor importance.

These three factors help in explaining how 23 million persons could be poor after receiving transfers in 1973. But *the most important explanation by far is that a large fraction of the total transfers is not counted as income at all.* In-kind programs that subsidize the consumption of particular goods and services (like food stamps, medicare, medicaid, and public housing) statistically make no contribution to alleviating poverty at all since the official poverty lines are defined in terms of *money* incomes. More than half of all federal transfers to those who remained poor after receiving transfers were in-kind.[20] I estimate that about 40 percent of the gross transfer to the entire bottom quartile was in the form of in-kind transfers. This means that the net *money* income per capita in the bottom quartile was only $1,060. An average family of four with a net money income of $4,240 would still be slightly below its poverty line. The exclusion of in-kind transfers, then, in conjunction with the other factors mentioned, can easily explain how 23 million persons remained *officially* poor after receiving transfers.

But is it reasonable to exclude in-kind transfers? It clearly is not. At the time when the official definitions of poverty were being formulated, in-kind transfers (except for education) were of negligible importance. It made sense to assume at that time that poor people would have to use money to purchase food, housing, and medical care. Now that many of the poor are, in effect, given these goods, consistency with the original conception of poverty requires that we either include in-kind transfers as income or reduce the money poverty lines to reflect the lower cost of subsidized goods. The former method is used in Table 2-8. In my view, the average net income of $1,812 per capita (which includes in-kind transfers except for education) is the relevant figure for considering the true level of well-being of the low-income population.

Education expenditures are excluded from in-kind transfers for a special reason. When the official poverty lines were constructed in the early 1960s, public schools were readily available at no direct money cost to the poor. Therefore, it is reasonable to assume that the official definitions took account of this particular in-kind transfer. But other in-kind transfers were unimportant at that time. In 1960, only about 5 percent of federal transfers were in-kind, but by 1973 that figure had risen to 24 percent.[21] In addition, in-kind transfers are more heavily concentrated on low-income families than cash transfers. Since in-kind transfers have expanded much more rapidly than cash transfers since 1965, it is understandable that very little impact was made on poverty defined by money income alone. But if it is reasonable to include in-kind transfers (except for education) in the income figures, Table 2-8 suggests that, on average, poverty became virtually nonexistent in the United States in 1973.

Further insight into the impact of redistribution on the low-income population can be obtained from an examination of Table 2-9. The figures in the first seven rows, which are from the Department of Health, Education and Welfare, give total federal outlays benefiting the poor by program categories for selected years. The "poor" referred to are those still officially poor *after* receipt of all government transfers. As the table shows, total federal transfers to the after-transfer poor quadrupled between 1964 and 1975, rising from $7.9 billion to $32.2 billion. The increase in the benefits per poor person is even more impressive since the number of poor persons declined during this period from 36.1 million in 1964 to 23.0 million in 1973. On a per capita basis, federal transfers increased more than fivefold between 1964 and 1973, rising from $219 to $1,139.

In addition to the impressive growth in total federal outlays, there has also been a significant shift in the relative importance of cash and in-kind transfers. (HEW distinguishes between in-kind transfers on food and housing, on the one hand, and outlays on

Table 2-9

FEDERAL OUTLAYS BENEFITING THE POOR, SELECTED FISCAL YEARS, 1964–1975

	1975 (estimate)	1973	1969	1966	1964
Federal outlays ($ billions)					
Cash payments	13.7	11.1	8.2	7.1	6.4
Food and housing transfers	5.4	3.5	0.7	0.3	0.3
Education	2.2	1.9	1.2	0.6	0.1
Health	6.8	5.4	3.5	0.8	0.7
Manpower	2.3	2.5	1.4	0.9	0.2
Other	1.8	1.9	0.9	0.5	0.2
Total	32.2	26.2	15.9	10.3	7.9
Total federal cash transfers ($ billions)	13.7	11.1	8.2	7.1	6.4
Total federal in-kind transfers ($ billions)	18.5	15.1	7.7	3.2	1.5
In-kind as percent of total	57	58	48	31	19
Number of poor persons	NA	23.0	24.1	28.5	36.1
Federal transfer per poor person (dollars)	NA	1,039	660	361	219

Source: U.S. Department of Health, Education and Welfare, Office of the Assistant Secretary for Planning and Evaluation, Office of Program Systems, "Federal Outlays Benefiting the Poor—Summary Tables," March 1974, Table 1 for the figures in the first seven rows. Other figures are the author's estimates.

education, health, manpower, and other programs on the other. All of these, however, are varieties of in-kind transfers applied to different goods.) [22] Total in-kind transfers were only $1.5 billion in 1964, or 19 percent of total outlays benefiting the poor. By 1973 in-kind transfers had risen to $15.1 billion, or 58 percent of a much enlarged total. The most significant growth in federal outlays has occurred precisely for those programs which do not contribute to the alleviation of poverty as officially defined.

Now we shall examine the 1973 figures more closely to compare the total value of resources (including in-kind transfers) available to the poor with the amount necessary to raise the poor to their poverty lines. The total income necessary to give every family that was officially poor in 1973 a sum equal to its poverty line was $30.5 billion.[23] The federal government actually transferred $26.2 billion to the poor in 1973. In other words, the federal transfer alone provided, on average, an amount equal to 86 percent of each family's poverty line.

But the poor also had resources available from state and local governments and, in addition, many poor families had earnings and other forms of income. I estimate the pretransfer income (mainly earnings) of the poor at $6 billion [24] and state and local government transfers (excluding education) at $7.4 billion.[25] The total value of resources available to the poor was thus $39.6 billion, which compares to the $30.5 billion calculated as necessary to raise each family to its poverty line. Therefore, the total value of the resources consumed by the poor in 1973 was enough to raise every officially poor family 30 percent above its poverty line.[26] The picture is very different, however, if in-kind transfers are not counted. I estimate that the total *money* income of the poor (assuming that half of state and local transfers were in-kind) was $20.8 billion in 1973, almost $10 billion below their combined poverty lines.[27]

That 23 million people were officially regarded as poor in 1973 was not due to a lack of resources but, rather, to the fact that $18.8 billion of in-kind transfers were not counted as income. These figures do not mean, however, that if in-kind transfers had been counted in 1973 no family would have been below its poverty line. Some, no doubt, would still have been, but that would be attributable to a maldistribution of transfers among the poor and not to an inadequate volume of transfers. Also, it should be emphasized that I am not implying that there is necessarily too much redistribution to low-income families. Whether poverty lines should be adjusted upward or downward is a different question from whether in-kind transfers should be counted. I have only argued that in-kind transfers should be counted and have then shown that, when they are, more than enough resources were being redistributed to the poor in 1973 to move everyone above the poverty line.

The HEW figures tend to support our earlier estimates of the volume of redistribution to the entire lowest quartile. Taking those figures and my estimates of state and local transfers, the total transfer per poor person was $1,461 in 1973. This makes plausible our earlier estimate of a net transfer of $1,248 per person for the entire lowest quartile in 1973.[28] To get an overall average of $1,248, with a figure of $1,461 for the officially poor, would require an average net transfer of about $1,100 for the remainder of those in the lowest quartile. It is, I think, quite reasonable to suppose that this was the case.[29]

The exclusion of in-kind transfers also largely accounts for the failure of the share of total money income received by the poorest quintile of families to show much improvement in recent years. According to Census Bureau figures, the lowest quintile had 4.8 percent of total money income in 1960 and that share had risen only to 5.5 percent by 1973. For 1960 and earlier years the exclusion of in-kind transfers made no great difference since programs of this type were quantitatively unimportant at that time. Counting in-kind transfers in 1960 would have raised the share of the lowest quintile from 4.8 percent to perhaps 5.0 or 5.5 percent. But when in-kind transfers are added to the money income figures for 1973, the estimated share of the lowest quintile reaches about 8.0 percent.[30]

Thus, contrary to the views of some commentators, there has been a dramatic improvement in the relative position of the lowest quintile. The adjusted share of income going to the lowest quintile rose from about 5.0 percent in 1960 to 8.0 percent in 1973. This represents a 60 percent improvement in the relative position of the poorest fifth of families. Stated differently, when in-kind transfers are counted, the average income of families in the lowest quintile was about 25 percent of the average for all families in 1960, but had risen to 40 percent of average family income in 1973.

One final remark concerning in-kind transfers. This analysis has valued in-kind transfers at their market value. But it is possible that such transfers are worth less to recipients than their market value, and it could be argued that only a fraction of the cost of these transfers should count as a measure of the benefits to the recipients. No attempt at such an adjustment has been made here, since it is not clear how large an adjustment would be required. (For a discussion of matters related to this point, see the section on in-kind transfers in the next chapter.)

Dependency among Low-Income Families?

One often stated goal for the welfare system is to encourage low-income families to become self-supporting. We need a system, it is said, that will ultimately make welfare unnecessary. Whatever the political value of such rhetoric or the intent of welfare legislation, it is clear that the design of almost all existing programs encourages people to become less self-supporting rather than more.[31] Moreover, there is some tentative evidence that suggests low-income families are becoming increasingly dependent on government as a source of income.

Table 2-8 showed that net government transfers have become an increasingly large percentage of total income of the lowest quartile over recent years. This fact, however, must be interpreted with care. It does not necessarily mean that low-income families are working or earning less: if pretransfer incomes remain unchanged while transfers increase, transfers as a percent of income will rise. Presumably, this is the intention of the redistribution. But it is also possible that when transfers increase, people will work less since there is less need to provide for one's own support. Economic theory predicts this type of response, at least for programs of the kind currently being used.

It would be helpful if, in the distribution of money income by quintiles (Table 2-2), income shares could be broken down into transfer income and other income. This would allow us to see if the share of income from earnings has declined for the lower quintiles in recent years. Unfortunately, the Census Bureau does not provide this type of breakdown. It does, however, supply some information concerning labor supply for the various quintiles. Table 2-10 contains several measures related to labor supply for the years 1953, 1963, and 1973. As can be seen there was a marked decline in labor supply in the lowest quintile between 1953 and 1973. Roughly, these figures suggest a decline of about 20 to 25 percent in labor supply since 1953. The same general pattern can be seen in the second quintile, but the decline is more moderate, perhaps 10 percent. In contrast, there appears to be little significant change for the top three quintiles, and perhaps even a slight increase due to an increase of about 18 percent in the average number of earners per family.

It should be stressed that it is not the absolute size of the figures in Table 2-10 that is important, but the change that has occurred. It is to be expected that the lowest quintile will have lower employment, since many aged families, female-headed families, and disabled persons are in this quintile. However, the reduction in labor supply over the period would not normally be expected.

These figures do not show that larger government transfers caused the decline in labor supply. Major demographic changes could have occurred which would have produced these results even in the absence of the increase in transfers.[32] I do not know if that is the case. Whatever the cause, it does appear that families in the lowest two quintiles, and especially the lowest, are relying less on work effort to provide income than they did in the past.[33] If this trend continues, the social and political problems it will raise could be tremendous.

Conclusion

It should be clear that the estimates of the net transfers to the lowest quartile in the income distribution are fairly rough. None-

Table 2-10

SELECTED LABOR SUPPLY CHARACTERISTICS OF FAMILIES AT VARIOUS INCOME LEVELS, 1973, 1963, AND 1953

	Lowest Quintile			Second Quintile			Average of Top Three Quintiles		
	1973	1963	1953	1973	1963	1953	1973	1963	1953
Mean number of earners	0.85	1.0	1.03	1.46	1.41	1.34	2.0	1.83	1.71
Head of family employed (percent)	40.7	47.8	57.6	71.3	74.7	80.5	89.1	89.7	89.7
Head of family did not work (percent)	48.9	40.2	NA*	18.7	15.3	NA*	5.1	5.3	NA*
No income from earnings (percent)	38.7	28.5	21.5	9.2	6.3	3.7	1.5	0.8	0.7

* Not available; for 1960 the figures were 36.2, 12.7, and 4.3.

Source: U.S. Bureau of the Census, "Money Income in 1973 of Families and Persons in the United States," *Current Population Reports*, series P-60, no. 97 (1975), Table 17.

27

theless, they are supported by HEW's estimates of federal transfers to the poor. But even these data are not likely to be very accurate, so the final estimates should not be considered overly precise. To go from the net transfer to a more detailed breakdown within the lowest quartile is even more hazardous. In fact, it is obvious that our knowledge of the distributional effects of government policies leaves much to be desired. The necessary data are simply not available. The main reason for this is the enormous number of separate programs that affect the distribution of income. One of the costs of relying on a large number of programs is that it becomes almost impossible to determine their net effect accurately.

In addition to recognizing the lack of precision in the estimates, there are two other qualifications that should be noted. First, governments affect the distribution of income in ways other than taxing and spending—for example, by minimum wage laws. Second, the estimates refer to redistribution within a given year. It is possible that if we could estimate the net effect on the distribution of lifetime incomes, the net redistribution would appear to be smaller. I have not tried to take account of these two factors, and believe they are not important enough to materially affect our main conclusions.

Our estimate of a large net redistribution in favor of the low-income population runs counter to the opinions of a great many economists. For example, Gordon Tullock, writing in 1971, states: "anybody examining the status of the poor in the modern world must realize that democracies do not make very large gifts to them." [34] He reiterated this opinion in 1974, with special reference to the United States.[35] Tullock is far from alone in this view. (I might mention that I shared this opinion until recently.) How could prevailing opinion be so wrong? In part, it is probably because the mushrooming of the welfare system has occurred in just the past few years, and most economists are not yet aware of how major a change has taken place. Studies published around 1970 often used data for 1966 (then perhaps the latest available), and even in the past two years a number of articles and books have appeared relying on data from the mid-1960s. The facts used in these studies are simply out of date, and so are opinions based on them. In addition, government adds to the confusion with its poverty tabulations showing that the number of poor persons has declined only slightly since 1966. That reinforces the misconception that society is not doing much for the poor. We have seen why these statistics are so misleading.

Another reason for the misconception is that many people generalize on the basis of only a small sub-set of government policies. Consider an observation made in a well-known 1969 article by Joseph Pechman, an authority on taxation: "It may be that, at some distant future date, the well-to-do and the rich will have enough income to satisfy not only their own needs, but also to help relieve the tax burdens of those who are less fortunate. In the meantime, the tax system will continue to disgrace the most affluent nation in the world." [36] Pechman was led to this judgment because he emphasized the tax system and largely ignored government expenditures. But, as we have seen, in 1973 government expenditures constituted a transfer to the low-income population that was four-and-a-half times the total taxes this population paid (Table 2-8). When both tax and expenditure policies are combined, the system is tilted heavily in favor of the low-income population.

With the hundreds of government policies, it is not surprising that some can be found which, examined in isolation, appear to work to the disadvantage of the poor. This is particularly true of taxes. Social security payroll taxes, sales taxes, excise taxes, and property taxes are often criticized because they are thought to be regressive. So-called tax "loopholes" have come in for especially harsh criticism. Philip Stern's recent best-seller is effectively subtitled "Why You Pay More While the Rich Pay Less" and has a chapter entitled "Uncle Sam's Welfare Program—for the Rich." [37] These descriptions are made to sound plausible by including a selective discussion of certain exclusions and deductions in the income tax law.

However difficult it may be, it is important to consider the welfare system in its entirety. This point will be repeatedly emphasized throughout the present study. In this chapter I have attempted to estimate the impact of *all* taxes and social welfare expenditures on the low-income population. Recognizing that the estimates are far from perfect, our main findings were:

First, the net redistribution in favor of the lowest quartile of the income distribution is huge and has grown very rapidly over the past six to eight years. In addition, in-kind transfers have grown much more rapidly than cash transfers.

Second, the net transfer (exclusive of education) to the lowest quartile is more than large enough to eliminate poverty as officially defined, if in-kind benefits are counted as income or if in-kind transfers are converted to cash transfers.

Third, some widely used government statistics concerning the low-income population have become increasingly unreliable over the past few years. Because the Census Bureau's statistics on income distribution and the official poverty counts ignore in-kind transfers, they are now largely useless as a basis for rational analysis of questions concerning income distribution.

Fourth, the low-income population appears to have become less self-supporting and more dependent on government transfers over the past two decades. This conclusion should be regarded as highly tentative until it is supported by other research.

CHAPTER III

ALTERNATIVE STRATEGIES FOR REDISTRIBUTION

As we have seen, the United States relies on a sizeable array of policies to benefit the poor. These policies are not all equally effective, and a constructive effort to reform the welfare system must begin with an understanding of their inherent limitations. A detailed analysis of all the actual and potential policies is not possible here. However, since almost all of the major policies in use, as well as the most important proposals for reform, fall into a few distinct categories, we can achieve our purpose by examining the major advantages and disadvantages of these basic policy categories.

Table 3-1 lists the major categories of policies that can be used in combating poverty and gives examples of each. Although this list is not complete—no list could include all the possibilities—

Table 3-1
ALTERNATIVE POLICIES FOR THE REDISTRIBUTION OF INCOME

Major Categories	Examples
I Cash transfers	
(a) Broad-based	Negative income tax, wage subsidy
(b) Categorical	AFDC, social security
II In-kind transfers	
(a) Consumption	Food stamps, public housing
(b) Human capital	Various training programs
III Special tax advantages	Personal exemptions in income tax laws, other "loopholes"
IV Direct intervention in markets	Minimum wage law, price ceilings

it covers most of the policies actually used in the United States and includes one category for which there is no U.S. program, namely, I(a), broad-based cash transfers. Strangely enough, the negative income tax, which falls in this category, is the policy favored by most economists.

This chapter analyzes each of these alternative types of policies, and then discusses the problems of relying simultaneously on a number of policies, as is currently being done. It is important to stress that our concern here is with the effects of alternative policies, not with how much redistribution is desirable. Any of these policies can be used to accomplish moderate or massive redistribution of income, but questions concerning the appropriate volume of redistribution differ substantially from those concerning the best way to carry out a given volume of redistribution. In effect, it is assumed in this chapter that society has decided to redistribute X billions of dollars and that the relevant question is what policies will do the job most effectively. The difficult problem of determining how much redistribution is desirable is then examined in Chapter 5.

Broad-Based Cash Transfers

A family is officially defined to be poor by the U.S. government when its money income falls below some specified figure. The most obvious way to alleviate poverty so defined is simply to give poor families money. In general, obvious methods for solving economic problems turn out, on examination, to have severe drawbacks. But in this case, many eminent economists have concluded that the obvious method is the preferred method and recommend dealing with poverty by giving poor people money. The negative income tax (NIT) is the name given to the type of cash transfer program most widely favored. It is not the only type of broad-based cash transfer, but it will serve to illustrate the important aspects of this type of program.

The NIT makes cash transfers to families, with the size of the transfer depending on the family's income and the number of members in the family. The distinguishing characteristic of the program is that, for families of a given size, the lower the income the larger the transfer. In other words, poorer families receive more money. Table 3-2 illustrates a hypothetical NIT. In this example, if pre-transfer income is zero the transfer is $2,500. At higher income levels the transfer is smaller, ultimately reaching zero at an income of $5,000. (It should be understood that these figures are for families of a given size. Normally, larger families would receive bigger benefits.)

Table 3-2

HYPOTHETICAL NEGATIVE INCOME TAX SCHEDULE

Pretransfer Income	Transfer	Total Disposable Income
$ 0	$2,500	$2,500
1,000	2,000	3,000
2,000	1,500	3,500
3,000	1,000	4,000
4,000	500	4,500
5,000	0	5,000

A program of this type can be concisely described by three policy variables. First is the *income guarantee*. This is the amount transferred to a family with a zero income. In our example, $2,500 is the income guarantee. The second policy variable is the *marginal tax rate*. The marginal tax rate determines by how much the transfer payment declines as pretransfer income rises. In Table 3-2, the transfer falls by $.50 when pretransfer income increases by $1. Thus, the marginal tax rate is 50 percent. If a family earned an extra $100, its net income would increase by only $50 since the transfer would fall by $50.

The third policy variable in an NIT plan is the *breakeven income*. This is the level of income at which the transfer is zero— $5,000 in our example. The breakeven income is determined by the income guarantee and the marginal tax rate. If the income guarantee is $2,500 and if the transfer declines by $.50 for each dollar of additional income, the transfer obviously becomes zero at an income of $5,000. Once the income guarantee and marginal tax rate are specified, the breakeven income is already determined since it equals the guaranteed income divided by the tax rate: $2,500/.5 = $5,000. Given this relationship, it is only necessary to specify two of the three policy variables to describe a particular NIT plan. We can describe the plan in Table 3-2 as a $2,500–50 percent NIT, giving only the income guarantee and marginal tax rate.

It would be something of an overstatement to say that these three variables fully describe an NIT. Normally, the transfer received by a family would also depend on family size, so we would need to give the income guarantee and tax rate for families of different sizes to provide a more complete description. In addition, it would be necessary to define what is to be counted in "pretransfer income." For example, would this be income before or after payment of taxes? The definition of income and treatment of families of different sizes are practical problems which we shall ignore for the moment since their resolution does not alter the basic characteristics of the program.

Even with these qualifications the NIT remains a very simple program. What are its advantages and disadvantages? While an adequate evaluation would require comparison with alternative policies, a brief listing of advantages includes the following:

(1) Assistance is objectively related to need. The fact of low income entitles a person or family to assistance.

(2) More assistance is given to those whose need is greater. An NIT concentrates funds on those with the lowest incomes.

(3) Assistance is in the form of cash. This maximizes the benefits to the recipient since he can purchase the goods that he values most highly.

(4) The NIT is a highly flexible policy instrument. Considerable control over the distribution of benefits can be achieved by modifying the definition of income or using graduated marginal tax rates.

Among the disadvantages of the NIT are:

(1) Money income does not adequately measure "need." Special circumstances, like heavy medical expenses, are not taken into account.

(2) Recipients of cash transfers are likely to spend the money on nonessentials. People are free to spend the taxpayers' money on liquor, drugs, entertainment, or tobacco.

(3) Transfers are made to people who are not poor. As long as the breakeven income is set above the poverty line some nonpoor families will receive transfers.

(4) The NIT treats the symptoms but not the causes of poverty. It does nothing to help the poor become self-supporting.

(5) The NIT undermines work incentives.

The question of work incentives has played a central role in efforts to reform welfare and therefore deserves special attention here. It is important to understand how a program may affect work incentives since programs other than the NIT may have this effect. An NIT affects a person's incentive to work in two ways. First, by providing assistance it reduces the necessity of supporting oneself. The recipients simply do not need to work as hard to attain any given level of total income. This is called the "income effect." Second, the NIT effectively reduces the net wage rate of recipients of transfers, which means that work does not pay as well. In the hypothetical NIT of Table 3-2, each additional $100 of earnings increases income by only $50 (since the transfer falls by $50), a result that is equivalent to a 50 percent reduction in the recipient's wage rate. This is the "substitution effect," a term that refers to a change in work effort produced by a change in relative prices (here the reduction in the net wage rate). Looked at another way, a person's total income falls by only $.50 for each $1 reduction in earnings, so the sacrifice involved in reducing work effort is decreased and it becomes less expensive to consume leisure (nonwork).

Both the income effect and the substitution effect of the NIT point to a reduction in work effort. Since all welfare programs that provide any assistance produce an income effect that is detrimental to work effort, attention has focused on the substitution effect. Under an NIT plan the substitution effect is directly linked to the marginal tax rate—the higher the marginal tax rate, the lower the net wage rate. If the marginal tax rate is 75 percent, for example, the transfer falls by $.75 for each $1 of earnings and the recipient's effective net wage rate is only one-fourth his market wage rate. In order to avoid major disincentive effects it is necessary that the marginal tax rate be kept reasonably low.

These arguments are the ones most commonly raised in evaluating the NIT, and they suggest the complexity of the issues that are involved. Evaluation of these arguments can be done adequately after the major alternative policies have been examined. For our present purposes, the NIT serves as a simple benchmark against which to compare the other types of policies that can be used to assist the poor.

Categorical Cash Transfers

Cash transfers made to members of certain demographic groups are called categorical. Some of the most important redistribution policies in the United States are of this type. They include such well-known programs as social security (for the aged), aid to families with dependent children (for families headed by women),[1] unemployment insurance (for the temporarily unemployed), and supplemental security income (for the aged poor, the disabled and the blind). Some other categories that have been singled out for special treatment include Indians (general assistance to Indians), Cuban refugees (assistance to Cuban refugees), and some surviving relatives of deceased coal miners (black lung survivors' benefits).

A fundamental question concerning categorical assistance is why some demographic groups should receive transfers but not others. One plausible answer is that the incidence of poverty is unusually high among particular groups. For example, among the aged, 54 percent have pretransfer incomes below their respective poverty lines. Among non-aged families headed by a female, 43 percent would be poor in the absence of transfers. By contrast, only about 10 percent of all other families have pretransfer incomes that place them in poverty.[2] Social security, supplemental security income (SSI), and AFDC make transfers to groups where low incomes are very prevalent.

But a high incidence of poverty in certain groups is hardly a compelling reason to restrict assistance to these groups. More than a fourth of all the pretransfer poor families do not belong to categories that entitle them to cash assistance. This excluded "category" includes primarily families headed by a working age male. A male who is young and poor receives no cash assistance, while a male who is old and poor is eligible for SSI and social security. Many argue that if our concern is with poverty, it is illogical to restrict benefits to poor people who fall in certain categories.

Not only do many poor people belong to demographic groups not covered by categorical programs, but also the categories that receive cash assistance include many who are not poor. Obviously, not all the aged or all the female-headed families are poor. The converse of the figures cited above is that 46 percent of the aged and 57 percent of female-headed families have pretransfer incomes above their poverty lines. Actually, as one would expect, there is a gradation of incomes within these categories from the very poor to the very wealthy, which means that categorical programs either will pay large benefits to many who are not poor, or will have to reduce benefits as income rises within a given category. Understandably, the latter alternative is generally chosen, so *categorical programs are essentially NIT programs restricted to certain demographic groups.* As we shall see, they have all the disadvantages of the NIT, together with several additional ones, but lack most of its advantages.

Although there seems a certain inequity in restricting transfers to poor people who happen to belong to certain population groups, there is an additional consideration that might provide a rationale for this treatment. It is frequently argued that the families in the major excluded group—those headed by a non-aged, non-disabled male—are able to support themselves if only they try, whereas that is generally not true for the aged, the disabled, or female-headed families. The implied distinction is between the deserving poor (who cannot, for some reason beyond their control, work to support themselves) and the undeserving poor (who are poor because they do not put forth enough effort). If valid, this distinction would provide a basis for a categorical approach. Granting benefits to those who cannot support themselves raises no problems regarding work incentives. The aged poor, as Bradley Schiller puts it, "require no work incentive provisions." [3] Moreover, denial of benefits to those who can work provides the strongest incentive of all: the threat of starvation if they do not work.

The difficulty is that the existing categorical programs do not neatly divide the population into those able and those unable to support themselves. Consider the kinds of persons covered by existing programs. Are the aged unable to work? About 25 percent of men sixty-five years of age and over are members of the labor force, and this figure greatly understates the percentage who are physically capable of working. As recently as the late 1940s nearly half of the aged male population was in the labor force. The fact that three-fourths of this group does not work today is often evidence not of inability to work but of a voluntary choice to substitute leisure for work and live on private pensions, public pensions, and accumulated assets.[4] Are families headed by females unable to work? A recent study prepared by Vee Burke and Alair Townsend for the Joint Economic Committee contains a section revealingly entitled "Formerly 'Unemployable' Groups Are Entering the Labor Force." The study points out that among fatherless families with preschool children, almost one-half of the mothers work; in addition, more than 40 percent of women receiving benefits under AFDC worked part of the year.[5] Are families receiving unemployment compensation unable to support themselves? Martin Feldstein reports that 83 percent of the benefits go to families with incomes above $5,000.[6]

So it is, at best, a serious oversimplification to argue that the population groups covered by categorical programs are unable to support themselves. What about those not covered? While it is certainly true that most of the adults in these groups are able to work, are they able to earn incomes that are above the poverty line? It is easy to think of many instances where male-headed families, despite their best efforts, remain poor. People whose skills are not highly valued in labor markets can remain poor even if they work full time. In fact, in 1970 more than one million families were poor despite full-time work all year long by the head of the family. A father with three or more dependents, for example, will still be poor if he works full time for forty hours a week at the legally established minimum wage rate. Many people work at even lower wage rates in sectors of the economy not covered by minimum wage laws. Further, for various reasons, some people can work only part time:

almost 2 million members of poor families worked for part of the year in 1970. In all, nearly 60 percent of the family heads of poor families worked either part or full time in 1970. Nor is it clear that we should consider all those who do not work as "undeserving." What about a man whose skills have become obsolete due to technological change? Or one who is involuntarily unemployed because of recession, the unemployment effects of the minimum wage law, or other factors?

Existing categorical programs do not neatly segregate the population into those who can and those who cannot support themselves. Fundamentally, this is because it is impossible to do this in any accurate way. The reasons why a family may be unable to support itself are too numerous and too little understood to serve as a basis for a rational poverty policy. Furthermore, the ability to support oneself is not an all-or-nothing characteristic: many can support themselves partially. The complexity and variety of circumstances leading to families' having very low incomes do not lend themselves to a simple categorical approach.

We have already noted that the categorical assistance programs enjoy the same disadvantages as the NIT. One, the work disincentive problem, deserves special mention. Under AFDC, benefits fall by 67 cents for each dollar of earnings beyond the first $30 each month, which means the program imposes an implicit marginal tax rate of 67 percent. (There is also wide variation in this tax rate from state to state, inasmuch as the program is administered by states and each welfare office has considerable discretion.) Both SSI and social security use tax rates of 50 percent beyond fairly low levels of earnings. Since female heads of families and aged persons are not unable to work, these high effective tax rates raise the same problems as does the tax rate in the NIT. Exactly how important a deterrent to work effort these programs have been is not known.

Perverse incentive effects are not limited to work effort. A particularly notorious example of a serious incentive problem is afforded by the impact of AFDC on family stability. The AFDC program generally restricts payments to families with female heads. Often this means that a father can support his wife and children best by deserting them, or appearing to do so. This is particularly true in the case of states with high AFDC payments and of men whose employment opportunities are limited. It is disconcerting to think that a government program would encourage families to break up, but a recent study by Marjorie Honig provides evidence that AFDC has had that effect: "The data imply . . . that independent of other factors, the size of the AFDC payment itself was an important determinant of family dissolution." The magnitude of the effect is distressingly large: "The 1960 figures indicate that the independent effect of a 10 percent higher AFDC stipend was to raise by 3-4 percent the share of families headed by women." Honig is careful to emphasize, however, that the vast majority of AFDC families became female-headed families for reasons other than to become eligible for welfare.[7]

A categorical approach will always give people an incentive to acquire the characteristics that make them eligible for that program. In the case of some programs, such as those that provide payments to the aged, this is not easy to do. But in the case of others it is often possible, as the AFDC example shows. For instance, a program that covers those who lack skills or education will encourage people to drop out of school and avoid job training. A program that covers the unemployed, like unemployment insurance, encourages people to remain unemployed instead of actively seeking work.[8] A program restricting benefits to poor families with children, as Nixon's proposed Family Assistance Plan would have, will encourage poor families to have children.

In a broad sense, all transfer programs must identify "categories" to receive aid. The question is to determine reasonably acceptable categories. The NIT relies primarily on the "category" of income below the plan's breakeven income. There is no doubt this would mean that some "undeserving" people would receive transfers. But this is also true of all the present categorical assistance programs. On the other hand, the NIT would cover all the "deserving" poor since it would cover everyone with a low income. Until an objective and acceptable way to distinguish between deserving and undeserving can be found, the broader treatment at least has the advantage of avoiding much of the arbitrary discrimination of present categorical programs. What else but discrimination by age is it to say that a poor male age sixty-four deserves no assistance, but that an equally poor male age sixty-five can receive aid under supplemental security income? What else but discrimination by race is it to grant assistance to poor Indians, but not to poor Mexican-Americans? Discrimination by income class is inherent in the NIT, just as it is in the federal income tax, but that is widely accepted as fair in the design of a welfare program.

In-Kind (Consumption) Transfers

A wide variety of government programs provides assistance by financing consumption of particular goods or services. Food stamps, medicare, medicaid, and public housing are among the best known programs of this type. As noted in Chapter 2, in-kind transfer programs have grown very rapidly over the past several years. This growth will accelerate if energy "coupons" or some form of national health insurance is enacted. It is particularly important, therefore, to analyze the consequences of this type of program.

The following analysis of two in-kind programs, food stamps and public housing, highlights the most important factors encountered in evaluating in-kind transfers. It should be noted that the specific provisions of in-kind transfer programs vary, so generalizations can be made only with great care. For example, eligibility requirements for the food stamp and public housing programs emphasize low incomes, while participation in medicare is restricted largely to the aged. Medicare and several other programs, like the Indian housing improvement program, combine the categorical and in-kind approaches.

Food Stamps. Eligibility for the food stamp program depends primarily on family size and income.[9] A family of four is eligible if it has an annual income below $6,800, after deductions for such items as housing and utility costs in excess of 30 percent of income.[10] Participation in the program means that the family can purchase food stamps at a price below their market value. Food stamps themselves can be thought of as checks signed by the government valid only for the purchase of specified food items. For example, if a family of four has an adjusted income of $3,000, it can purchase $1,800 worth of food stamps for a price of $852. The difference between the market value of the stamps (the coupon allotment) and the purchase price is the amount of the government transfer to the family. Thus, in this case the government is paying 53 percent of the cost of the family's consumption of $1,800 worth of food.

It is important to emphasize that the value of the food stamps a family can purchase depends only on family size. All eligible families of four can purchase $1,800 worth of food stamps and no more. They can, however, supplement their food consumption by buying additional food at the market price with their own funds. On the other hand, a variable purchase option allows families to purchase less than $1,800—specifically, either one-fourth, one-half, or three-fourths of the basic coupon allotment. Very few participants in the program make use of this option; most elect to purchase the $1,800 basic allotment. It is not an oversimplification, then, to say that the food stamp program establishes a floor of $1,800 in food consumption for a family of four.

While all participating families of the same size are eligible to purchase the same basic coupon allotment, the price they must pay depends on the family's adjusted income. A family of four with a zero income receives its $1,800 in food stamps free (a purchase price of zero). At higher income levels the purchase price is increased. Table 3-3 provides a convenient summary of how the program (as of July 1974) affects families at different income levels. Ignoring the variable purchase option, all four-person families that participate in the program, regardless of income, will purchase $1,800 in food stamps and presumably consume at least this amount of food (although there are illegal ways to get around this). The transfer is the difference between the coupon allotment and the purchase price. At an income of $1,000 the purchase price is $228 ($1,800 − $1,572), and the purchase price of the same coupon allotment increases steadily with income to reach $1,512 ($1,800 − $288) at an income of $6,000. The total value of resources available for consumption (omitting certain expenditures allowed in excess of this amount) is shown in the third column, but consumption of food must account for at least $1,800 of this total.

Table 3-3 makes it clear that the food stamp program is in effect an NIT program that restricts the way the recipient can spend his total income. For a family of four it provides an income guarantee of $1,800, with the proviso that at least that amount be spent on food. The transfer falls as income rises, but at all income levels

Table 3-3

FOOD STAMP BENEFITS FOR A FAMILY OF FOUR

(as of July 1974)

Pretransfer Adjusted Income	Transfer	Total Adjusted Income	Minimum Food Consumption (Coupon allotment)
$ 0	$1,800	$1,800	$1,800
1,000	1,572	2,572	1,800
2,000	1,308	3,308	1,800
3,000	948	3,948	1,800
4,000	660	4,660	1,800
5,000	444	5,444	1,800
6,000	288	6,288	1,800

Source: Kenneth W. Clarkson, *Food Stamps and Nutrition* (Washington, D. C.: American Enterprise Institute, 1975), Table 4.

minimum food consumption is specified at $1,800. The rate at which the transfer falls varies over the income level range, but the implicit marginal tax rate on net income is generally between 25 and 30 percent. Therefore, this program can be expected to affect work incentives in the same way as the NIT.[11]

(In passing, it is interesting to note that the food stamp program is a more generous NIT—ignoring inflation—than President Nixon's ill-fated Family Assistance Plan. It will be recalled that the FAP involved an income guarantee of $1,600.)

Apart from work incentives, the major impact of the food stamp program is on the consumption patterns of recipients. Typically, the program leads to greater food consumption than would occur if the transfer were unrestricted. For example, suppose that families with incomes below $6,000 spend one-third of their incomes on food in the absence of restrictions. On this assumption, if a family with an income of $2,000 received an unrestricted transfer of $1,308, bringing its after-transfer income to $3,308, it would choose to spend $1,103 on food. But under the restriction of the food stamp program, the family would have to spend $1,800 on food, so it would consume $697 more food—and $697 less of other goods—than it would have chosen to consume if the subsidy had been in cash.

This distortion in the consumption patterns of participating families means that the subsidy under the food stamp program is worth less to the recipients than an equivalent amount of cash they could spend as they wished. The net benefit to a family is not equal to the transfer received because of the restriction on how it must spend its income. To put this point differently, if the same amounts were transferred, but in the form of unrestricted cash payments (as with the NIT), recipients would be better off at no extra cost to the taxpayers. Kenneth Clarkson has estimated that a transfer of $1 under the food stamp program is worth only $.82 to recipients on average.[12] In other words, if the food stamp program were converted to an unrestricted NIT, net benefits to recipients could be increased by about one-fourth (.18/.82) at no additional cost to taxpayers. And the increase would be even greater if the administrative costs of the food stamp program were larger than those of an NIT, which is almost surely the case.

The size of the distortion in consumption patterns varies with income, as Clarkson emphasizes. In general, the distortion is greater at lower levels of income because $1,800 represents greater "overconsumption" of food for families with lower incomes. For example, at a pretransfer income of $1,000, the family is forced to consume $943 more food than it would consume if it could spend the $1,572 transfer as it wished (still assuming one-third is the preferred proportion of income to devote to food). So the net benefit is a smaller percentage of the transfer to the lowest income families than it is to families at higher income levels. Tragically, the restriction that the transfer be spent on food consumption is most harmful to those who are neediest. It may not be harmful at all to those with higher incomes since it may be ineffective. If a family with a pretransfer income of $5,000 were given an unrestricted transfer of $444, it would end up spending $1,815 on food. Under the food stamp program it would purchase $1,800 of food with the food stamps and an additional $15 with cash. Therefore, at higher income levels the food stamp program has the same effect on consumption as an NIT of the same size.

Of course, it can be argued that it is desirable to distort consumption in favor of food. We will look at this point after examining public housing since basically the same arguments are applicable to that program, and to the other in-kind transfers as well.

Public Housing. Public housing is a more complex program than food stamps. It is administered by local housing authorities (which are agents of municipal governments) and is heavily subsidized by the federal government. In addition to determining the distribution of the housing units among recipients, the local housing authorities plan and direct the construction of public housing units. Thus, the government is involved in the production of the good being subsidized, in contrast to the food stamp program where the government role is limited to financing the consumption of privately produced food. One effect of government involvement in production can be summarized briefly: it costs the government significantly more to produce housing units than it does private producers. Richard Muth, for example, estimates that the government's "expenditures per dwelling are about 20 percent more than private producers would make for dwellings of the same rental value." [13] John Kraft's and Edgar Olsen's estimate is of similar magnitude.[14]

Apart from the production aspects of public housing, the program dispenses benefits to recipients in a way not dissimilar to the food stamp program. Eligibility depends on income, but the cut-off points vary from locality to locality. Those admitted to public housing are charged a rent that is below the market value of the unit, just as food stamp recipients are charged a purchase price below the market value of the stamps. The rents are determined by the local housing authorities, so rent policies also vary among localities. Moreover, as in the case of food stamp recipients, there is a federal limit on what public housing tenants can be charged: housing authorities cannot charge tenants more than 25 percent of their income in rent. Assuming this limit is the amount charged to a particular tenant, an effective marginal tax rate of 25 percent is imposed because if the tenant's income rises, one-fourth of the increment is paid in increased rent for the same dwelling unit. Again, the similarity to an NIT, in this case with a restriction that the subsidy be spent on housing, is striking.

By denying the recipients the freedom to spend the government subsidy as they please, the public housing authority also distorts consumption patterns. Kraft and Olsen estimate that, on average, a public housing subsidy (the difference between rents and market value) of $101 per month confers benefits of only $76 per month due to this distortion. Thus, if unrestricted cash transfers were made instead, the subsidies would be worth one-third more to the recipients. The impact in terms of creating waste by distorting consumption patterns is apparently of about the same magnitude as it is in the food stamp program.

There is one major difference in the way food stamps and public housing affect consumption. Food stamps always lead to the consumption of food in amounts that are either greater than or equal to the consumption that would occur under unrestricted cash transfers. Paradoxically, public housing can lead to less consumption of housing than would an equal-cost unrestricted cash transfer. The reason for this is that it is very expensive, if not impossible, for public housing recipients to consume more housing than the fixed quantity made available by the housing authority. Suppose, under a public housing program, that a family is offered a two-bedroom apartment but would prefer, given the same subsidy, a three-bedroom apartment. The family may decide to live in the two-bedroom public housing apartment, since its only alternative would be to forego the subsidy. The family obviously cannot build an additional bedroom, although it might be willing to pay the additional cost of a three-bedroom apartment if it could do so without losing the subsidy. (This is exactly the same reason why public schools may reduce consumption of schooling for some people.) [15]

It might be thought that the possibility of underconsumption of housing is of little importance—just an interesting curiosity. However, Kraft and Olsen have found that an amazing 49 percent of their sample of public housing tenants were consuming less housing than they would under a program of equal-cost cash transfers.[16] They caution that their sample is not typical of all public housing recipients (families in their sample have somewhat higher incomes and more children than the average), so that their finding is not a reliable estimate for all recipients. Still, the peculiar effects found for some recipients forcefully demonstrate that the program is not even well designed to increase housing consumption.

One other important difference between food stamps and public housing concerns the coverage of the program. Everyone who is eligible for food stamps (that is, has a low enough income) can receive them. Although only 30 to 40 percent of the eligible group is participating, this is due to lack of knowledge or a belief that the benefits are not worth the cost (including the time-consuming process of establishing eligibility) rather than to restrictions on the supply of funds.[17] But under public housing only a small proportion of those with low enough incomes to qualify can be accommodated, given the limited supply of public housing units. Muth estimated that, in 1960, only 7 percent of those eligible were receiving benefits. While the figure may be higher now, only 5 percent of households with annual incomes below $5,000 were living in public housing in 1972.[18]

The excess demand for public housing units, manifested in long waiting lists in most cities, raises serious problems of fairness. Since there are not enough public housing units for all those who are eligible, on what basis will it be decided that some will get sizeable subsidies and others will get nothing? That decision is ultimately made by the local housing authorities. But in order to see how the structure of this program can often yield untoward results, consider the following situation. Suppose the housing authority is having budgetary problems. It cannot raise rents if it is already charging tenants 25 percent of their incomes in rent. But it can replace low-income tenants with higher-income tenants, and this will increase the total rent received by the housing authority. I do not suggest that favoring higher-income households is typical behavior of housing authorities, but this plausible example indicates the types of pressures that may influence the discriminatory judgments that must be made. It may be worth mentioning in this connection that 18 percent of all households in public housing have incomes above $5,000.

Evaluation of Arguments for In-Kind Transfers. The food stamp and public housing programs have been used to illustrate the effects of in-kind transfers. Not all of the effects noted are necessary consequences of this approach; some could be avoided with appropriate reforms. But distortion in consumption patterns—that is, the overruling of recipients' preferences—is an almost unavoidable effect of in-kind transfers. There are serious arguments that stress the desirability of this effect. We now turn to an evaluation of the most common of these arguments.

One common argument for an in-kind transfer goes something like this: "The poor cannot afford to pay for adequate housing—or food, or medical care, or health insurance, et cetera—so it is up to the government to ensure the availability of these things." This familiar point is so vague that it provides no reason for favoring a housing subsidy over a cash transfer. A cash transfer would enable the recipient to purchase more housing as well as more of other goods. The major reason why the poor have inadequate housing, medical care, and food is that their spendable incomes are low. Give them money and these specific symptoms of low incomes would be alleviated. A tenable case for an in-kind transfer in preference to a cash transfer must establish that the recipient of cash transfers would consume too little of some goods *and* too much of others, since the effect of an in-kind transfer is simply to restrict the way the recipient would spend the transfer if it were unrestricted.

It might be argued that the poor are incapable of looking after their own needs. Left to themselves, they would spend too much on liquor, tobacco, movies, and so on but not enough on goods they "really" need, like housing, medical care, and food. This paternalistic argument is a tenable defense of the in-kind approach. For that matter, it can be used to rationalize just about any interference in people's affairs, so we must be very careful before we use it to justify programs costing billions of dollars and affecting millions of people.

The paternalistic motivation for in-kind transfers seems to envision a government agency composed of experts who will objectively evaluate each family's needs and make sure the appropriate quantity and quality of goods is consumed. Actually, existing programs are a far cry from this vision. Food stamps simply place a floor of $1,800 under food consumption for a family of four. That floor does not take account of the ages, sexes, or weights of family members, special dietary needs, the capability of the family chef, or of other needs that may be even more pressing than food. This is more of a meat-ax approach than the careful tailoring of consumption to needs. Even so, it is still conceivable that the food stamp program leads to better diets on average. Here, however, the evidence is surprising. Although the program increases food consumption, it apparently does not lead to more *nutritious* diets. Recipients consume more palatable or easier to prepare foods, but not foods that are more nutritious.[19]

It is difficult to defend the food stamp program as a vehicle for improving the nutrition of poor families. To accomplish that objective, the program would have to require much more detailed regulation of consumption by recipients than it does. Before accepting a drastic policy like that, let us consider the fundamental question: would the poor spend too little of their incomes on important items in the absence of restrictions?

Table 3-4 shows the percentages of consumer expenditures that families at different income levels devoted to food, housing, and medical care in 1960. Families with incomes below $3,000 (equivalent to about $4,500 in 1973 prices) were voluntarily devoting 72 percent of their budgets to these items. This amount was considerably above the ratios for middle-income families (60.4 percent) and high-income families (55.3 percent). Apparently, the poor do not need to be forced to devote most of their budgets to the "necessities": they simply cannot afford not to.

It is still possible to argue that 72 percent is too low. But this must mean that the poor spend too high a percentage on some other goods. What are these goods? They spend 7.1 percent on clothing and 8.6 percent on transportation. Such amounts hardly seem too high. What about alcohol, tobacco, and recreation? The poor spend

Table 3-4

PERCENTAGE DISTRIBUTION OF FAMILY EXPENDITURES, BY INCOME CLASS, 1960

	Money Income Class		
Category	Under $3,000	$5,000 to $7,499	$15,000 and over
Food	29.4	24.7	20.1
Housing a	34.4	29.1	29.1
Transportation	8.6	16.0	14.9
Medical care	8.5	6.6	6.1
Clothing	7.1	9.9	12.2
Recreation	2.3	3.8	4.7
Tobacco	2.1	2.0	1.1
Alcohol	1.0	1.5	1.9
Other	6.6	6.4	9.9

a Includes shelter and other home-related expenses.

Source: *Consumer Expenditures and Income: Survey Guidelines*, Bureau of Labor Statistics Bulletin 1684 (1971), pp. 104-105, Table B-17.

5.4 percent on all these categories together. Considering alcohol alone, the poor allocated 1 percent of their expenditures to this good, whereas the figure is 1.9 percent in the $15,000 and over class. In absolute terms, the average high-income family spent $242 per year on alcohol as compared with $21 per year for the low-income family.

I think one can conclude, then, that there is little need for the federal government to try to shift the consumption patterns of the poor in favor of food, housing, and medical care. The popular impression that the poor will waste the taxpayers' money if they are not compelled to spend it "wisely" is simply an improper generalization from a few notorious examples. There are certainly some cases where poor persons drink too much, but the important point is that these cases are atypical. Policies which affect millions of people should not treat the responsible ones, who are clearly in the overwhelming majority, as if they were irresponsible. By and large, I am sure that most poor families can look after their own needs better than a government agency would, if they are provided with adequate incomes.

Another line of argument supporting in-kind transfers is based on the economist's concept of externalities. An externality is said to exist when an action of one person or group directly affects (outside normal market relationships) the welfare of another person or group. Air pollution, for example, is an external cost of driving an automobile since exhaust emissions pollute the atmosphere other people breathe. It is claimed that the consumption of some goods by the poor generates external benefits, that is, directly benefits the nonpoor. Thus, immunization of some against a contagious disease will lower the probability that others will contract the disease. The crux of the argument is that the poor will underconsume goods generating external benefits because they will disregard the benefits flowing to other people. An in-kind transfer can induce them to consume more of that good, thereby conferring greater benefits on the nonpoor.

Housing, food, and medical care are frequently mentioned as goods that generate external benefits when consumed by the poor. Space does not permit an adequate evaluation of this complex argument, but a few points should be stressed.[20] First of all, it is not clear whether external benefits actually exist or, if they do, whether they are quantitatively important. The few attempts to measure *some* of the external benefits of public housing suggest that these effects are unimportant. Better housing apparently does not lead to a reduction in juvenile delinquency, for example.[21] Nor do public housing projects increase property values of surrounding property.[22] There may still be other, less tangible externalities, of course. But to a large extent the externality argument seems to degenerate into speculation that the nonpoor will feel better off simply knowing that the poor consume specific goods. Externalities seem to have become the excuse for governmental paternalism.

Rather than speculate on the existence of these external effects, let us simply assume that they exist. This still does not prove that in-kind transfers are preferable to cash transfers. Instead, it just implies that there exists some form of in-kind transfer that is more efficient than a cash transfer, but to find out what it is we must know the benefits to the poor and nonpoor of consumption by the poor. We do not have that information, nor is there any known way to get it. In any event, it is clear that existing in-kind transfers are not of the type that would be required to accurately take account of external benefits, assuming these benefits exist: recall that public housing reduces housing consumption for some recipients.

Furthermore, the case for in-kind transfers is weaker given the fact that a large part of the budgets of the poor are devoted to goods generating external benefits.[23] Since the poor spend 72 percent of their incomes on food, housing, and medical care, about that portion of a cash transfer would be spent on increased consumption of these goods.[24] It is not clear that the combined effects of three separate in-kind programs can be expected to do any better. (Even if they could, this would mean reduced expenditures on clothing and transportation, and it is not implausible that these goods also generate external benefits.)

To see why simultaneous use of several in-kind transfers tends to be self-defeating, consider the hypothetical case examined in Table 3-5. Assume that the poor prefer to spend one-third of their incomes on food and one-third on housing. A family with a $3,000

Table 3-5

COMBINED EFFECTS OF HYPOTHETICAL FOOD AND HOUSING SUBSIDIES

Pretransfer income	$3,000
Transfer in food program	900
Minimum food consumption	1,600
Transfer in housing program	900
Minimum housing consumption	1,600
Total consumption	4,800

income then receives a $900 transfer from a food stamp program that requires it to consume $1,600 in food. If this is the only transfer program used, the family will consume $300 more food than it would if given an unrestricted cash transfer. (It would spend one-third of $3,000 plus one-third of $900, or $1,300, on food in the latter case.) But now suppose a second program is used to stimulate housing consumption. If *only* the housing program is used, it too leads to $300 more consumption than would a $900 cash transfer. But when the two policies are used together, they transfer $1,800 to the family and it is consuming $1,600 each of food and housing. However, if the $1,800 were given in cash, the family would voluntarily spend one-third of its total income of $4,800 on food and one-third on housing. In other words, taken together the two in-kind transfers do not lead to greater consumption of food and housing than would a cash transfer, even though either program if used by itself would.

This example should suffice to indicate the difficulty of devising several programs which simultaneously lead to greater consumption (than would a cash transfer) of several goods that comprise an important part of the family's normal consumption expenditures. When the goal is to increase consumption of goods already accounting for 72 percent of the budget, the NIT is likely to do just as good a job as the type of in-kind programs currently in use.

Furthermore, we have ignored the fact that in-kind transfers typically involve higher administrative costs. Administrative costs are estimated to be at least 9 percent of the amount transferred under the food stamp program, and about 7 percent of the transfer under public housing.[25] For comparison, the NIT has been estimated to require an administrative cost of about 3 percent.[26] What this means is that the NIT can provide 4 to 6 percent more resources to the poor at no extra cost to taxpayers.

Finally, one other adverse effect of in-kind transfers deserves special emphasis. In-kind transfers will be preferred by the producers of the subsidized goods since these subsidies will redound partly to their benefit. Producer groups will clearly have an incentive to use their political power to shape the programs to their interests, as opposed to the interests of the recipients or the general public. This makes it unlikely that the political process will produce programs that are adapted to the needs of the recipients or the general public. An example of this is the rule that food stamps may not be used to purchase imported food. This rule shunts demand in favor of domestic food producers, to their advantage but not to the advantage of food stamp recipients or taxpayers. Another example is the Davis-Bacon Act requirement that public housing projects pay construction workers wages that are generally higher than market wages.[27] This inflates the cost of producing public housing units, with construction workers gaining at the expense of the general public. In general, in-kind transfers are simply an invitation to special interest groups to mold the programs to their advantage.

When compared with the way in-kind transfer programs have operated, the case for the NIT appears quite strong. In-kind transfers produce capricious interferences in consumer choices, require high administrative costs, create sizeable inequities, greatly complicate the system, and necessitate what appear to be totally arbitrary judgments about what goods to subsidize and how heavily to subsidize them. It is not clear that there are any important advantages to be had from using this approach to redistribution.

In-Kind (Human Capital) Transfers

Many people view training programs for equipping the poor with better job skills as an attractive alternative to income transfers. Subsidized training is, of course, simply a particular form of in-kind transfer, and the arguments for and against such transfers discussed above are therefore pertinent. In addition, several special considerations should be examined.

Training programs, both the on-the-job and off-the-job varieties, can be provided by private firms. If they are effective in augmenting earning capacity, the poor have an incentive to purchase this service simply because it represents a good investment for them. This reasoning suggests that it is not necessary for government to provide job-training programs since, if the training pays off, the poor already have an incentive to purchase it.

Several economists find a flaw in this argument. Since the poor do not have ready funds, they must borrow money if they are to purchase extensive training. But they have difficulty in borrowing money for this purpose because the only collateral they can offer is the uncertain prospect of higher future income, collateral few lending institutions will accept. Thus, the poor may not be able to improve their earning capacity even though it would be an economical investment to do so. This argument, pointing to a special problem in the workings of capital markets, suggests that job training may deserve special encouragement. However, no one knows if the argument is quantitatively important. And, in any case, it is not clear whether the encouragement should take the form of subsidizing loans to undertake training or outright government provision of training. Government is an inefficient producer of housing, as we have seen, and it is far from certain that it can do better than private producers in the case of training.

Whatever the rationale for this type of in-kind transfer, over the past decade the federal government has provided a bewildering variety of programs of remedial education, on-the-job training, off-the-job training, and counseling. These programs have all the defects typically associated with in-kind transfers, but this might be a modest price to pay if the programs were successful in substantially raising the earning capacity of trainees. Unfortunately, no one knows if they are. Despite numerous studies devoted to analyzing these programs, disagreement still exists concerning their effectiveness.[28]

It is understandable that there would be wide disagreement, for it is very difficult to determine how effective a training program has been. Many studies have found that the earnings of trainees increased immediately after completion of some program. But to justify the programs as a wise investment it is generally necessary that earnings remain higher for a number of years. Several of the studies in question have assumed that the higher earnings immediately following the program would persist for ten years and, on that assumption, benefits were estimated to exceed the costs. However, this assumption may be too optimistic. A follow-up study of a Job Corps program found that, after a year-and-a-half, the initial gain in earnings of $203 had declined to the point where the remaining gain was no longer statistically significant.[29] Whether this decline is typical is not known, but it underlines the difficulty in evaluating a program whose worth depends upon its having effects over a long period of time.

Even when earnings increase following training, it is not clear that this can be counted as a net gain. Some writers believe that these gains result from the job placement services of the programs (rather than from any increase in productivity of the trainees) that may place trainees in jobs other people would otherwise have gotten. In that case, the gain to the trainees is simply someone else's loss, and there is no net gain.

Still another set of problems bedevils attempts to generalize on the basis of program results. For example, the effectiveness of any training effort clearly depends on the ability and motivation of the trainees. In the main, the participants in past manpower training programs have been volunteers. It may be that those who volunteered were more receptive to training than those who did not. If so, expanded training programs would apply to trainees who would gain less from the experience than did the early volunteers.

In view of these problems and others too numerous to mention, trying to isolate the independent impact of a training program on the productivity of trainees is sure to remain a difficult task. What can be concluded from the evidence, however, is that we do not know why some programs have been more successful than others. Estimates of the ratio of benefits to costs vary from as much as fifteen for some programs (indicating a high degree of success) to well below one for others (indicating failure), although most estimates are above one. Indeed, studies of the same programs undertaken for different states often yield great differences. Given the highly uncertain results of these studies, and given that we do not know what characteristics account for a program's success or failure, it is hazardous to embark on expanded training programs as a means of combating poverty.

All of the studies referred to above have sought to measure effectiveness by comparing the earnings records of trainees with those of non-trainees. An alternative approach would be to see if training programs have had any noticeable effect on the aggregate income distribution statistics. Probably at least 10 million people were enrolled in training programs during the 1963-73 period (although not all who were enrolled completed the programs).[30] Assuming that these trainees were concentrated in the lower range of the income distribution, they would have constituted a sizeable fraction of the labor supply at lower income levels. (There were only 9.4 million earners in the poorest quintile of families in 1972.) If the results of the programs were at all significant, we would have expected to find an improvement in the share of total earnings accruing to the bottom 20 percent or 40 percent of the income distribution during that period. As we saw in the previous chapter, however, the *income* shares (earnings plus cash transfers) of the bottom two quintiles had not shown any noticeable improvement as of 1973. What had happened to the *earnings* shares was not clear, but some evidence suggested a slight drop over the past decade.

To repeat a caveat from the previous chapter, these aggregate data are somewhat suspect. Nonetheless, they certainly suggest that training programs have not had any substantial effect on the aggregate earnings of the bottom 20 percent of the income distribution. Certainly benefits do not generally exceed costs by a factor of ten, as studies of some of the programs suggested. If figures like these were correct, the earnings share of the bottom quintiles would surely have shown sizeable improvement. This does not prove that the government training programs were failures, since factors other than these programs influence the aggregate figures. Even so, I think one can conclude that we should not be too optimistic about the potential of manpower training programs for transforming the poor into highly productive workers.

Lowell Gallaway has recently developed an hypothesis with distressing implications for the efficacy of public policy in this area.[31] He contends that a person's "genetic human capital," roughly his "innate ability," is overwhelmingly the most important determinant of productivity and earnings:

> Specifically, if income differentials are largely the result of market valuations of genetic, i.e., "natural" differences between people, there is little that can be done from the standpoint of public policy to equalize income distribution through approaches intended to augment the human capital of low income individuals. Thus, emphasis on increasing formal education, job retraining, and the like, are not apt to produce substantial improvements in the relative economic status of low income people.[32]

Although Gallaway may have overestimated the importance of "genetic human capital," it may well be that training programs are very limited in what they can accomplish. Even if this judgment is unwarranted, as I hope, it will still remain necessary to put heavy reliance on income transfer programs. Some among the poor will always be unable to work, or able to work only part time, or unable to benefit from training sufficiently to remove them from poverty. For these people there is no viable alternative to an income transfer policy.

Special Tax Advantages

Many find it anomalous that families officially classified as poor by the U.S. government must pay taxes that drive them even more deeply into poverty. Yet poor families do pay many taxes, and these taxes take a substantial portion of their incomes. No one knows precisely what the average tax rate on the poor is, but most studies conclude that it is surprisingly high. Typically, estimates of the combined impact of federal, state, and local taxes on families with incomes below $3,000 vary between 25 and 40 percent.[33] Most studies find the average tax rate on the poor to exceed that for most other income levels except the very highest.

One popular method of helping the poor is to structure the tax system so that they pay a smaller share of the total burden while the nonpoor pay a larger share. This "redistribution of the tax burden" already influences the design of many federal and state tax laws. The federal government, for example, uses a personal exemption of $750 in the income tax. Another special provision, the low-income allowance, provides an additional deduction for poor families. Together, these provisions mean that a family of four pays no income taxes unless its income exceeds $4,300. A double exemption applies for the aged. In addition, most state income tax laws provide for exemptions, and several states exclude some "necessities" like food and drugs from sales taxes. Nevertheless, it is clear that the poor continue to pay substantial taxes.

Despite the popularity of special tax concessions for the poor, this approach has severe drawbacks when viewed as a policy to alleviate poverty. An obvious one is that most poor families would remain poor even if their taxes were reduced to zero. For example, assuming an effective tax rate of 25 percent, a family with a before-tax income of $2,000 has an after-tax income of $1,500. Obviously, even if all taxes on this family were eliminated, its income would still be far below the poverty line.

Perhaps of greater importance, the distributional effects of tax reductions are often extremely inequitable. Suppose that we eliminated all taxes (assumed to be 25 percent) on incomes below $4,000. This would increase the net income of those with $1,000 by only $250, but would aid those with $4,000 by $1,000. The larger gains invariably go to those who are better off to begin with. In addition, taxes would have to be reduced for families with incomes well above $4,000 to avoid serious incentive effects. Otherwise a family with an income of $4,500 would continue to pay $1,125, its burden at the 25 percent rate, while a family with an income of $4,000 would pay nothing. In other words, after-tax income would be higher for incomes of $4,000 (after-tax income of $4,000) than for incomes of $4,500 (after-tax income of $4,500 − $1,125 = $3,375). Not only would this be unfair, but also it would mean a marginal tax rate above 100 percent, with the serious disincentive effects that would imply. Therefore, the elimination of taxes on the first $4,000 of income would require a reduction in tax burdens for all families with incomes up to, probably, at least $7,000. The largest benefits would go to those with incomes near $4,000 and very little gain would go to those with the lowest incomes.

As serious as this limitation of special tax advantages obviously is, there is an even more fundamental problem associated with their use. To illustrate this problem, let us examine the effects of a specific proposal to reduce the burden of state and local taxes on poor families. The proposal is to use a federal tax credit for state and local taxes paid by the poor. This approach has the support of several economists;[34] in addition, President Nixon advocated a form of tax credit limited to the elderly during the 1972 presidential campaign.

A 100-percent tax credit for local taxes paid by those with incomes below $4,000—which we will use to illustrate the analysis—is very simple. If a family has local taxes of $250, then it subtracts $250 from its federal income tax liability. If it pays no federal income tax, as is likely, then the federal government simply makes a cash transfer of $250 to the family. In either case, the effect is to remove the burden of local taxes from the poor.

Apart from the equity issues, this proposal seems straightforward until we examine its probable effects on the political process that determines local expenditures and taxes. For one thing, under such a policy, how would the poor vote on questions of local government spending? Since every dollar in additional local taxes would be offset by a dollar in federal transfers, increases in local spending would cost the poor nothing. As long as the local programs were of any value, the poor would favor them. Thus the policy would have an expansionary effect on local government expenditures and, in turn, on local taxation.

Furthermore, the local government would have a strong incentive to place the entire burden of local taxes on the poor since the poor would be fully reimbursed by the federal government. That would benefit both the nonpoor and the poor at the expense of the general federal taxpayers, surely an unintended and undesirable outcome. Therefore, some limitation of the size of the tax credit would be essential. But that would probably eliminate most of the advantage of the tax credit to the poor. Suppose the limit were $500 and a poor family was initially paying $300 in taxes. If the local government had determined that a net burden of $300 was appropriate for this family, why would it not simply increase the family's nominal tax to $800? This would leave the family with a net burden of $300 as before ($800 less a $500 tax credit), and the local government would have increased its tax revenue by $500 at the expense of the federal government.

These extreme outcomes could be partly, but not fully, avoided by using a partial tax credit. The federal government could reimburse the poor for half of the local taxes paid, for instance. Even so, the incentive for the local government to expand its expenditures and increase the nominal tax burden of the poor would still be present, only in diminished intensity. The reason is that, whatever the size of the tax credit, the local government would be given the opportunity to have the federal government finance part of its increased expenditures. By levying heavier taxes on those entitled to the tax credit, part of the local tax burden could be shifted to the federal government.

These perverse effects of a tax credit indicate the dangers of tampering with tax schedules in an attempt to redistribute income. In a country with democratic political institutions, it is important that all persons of voting age pay taxes. To exempt some persons is to tempt them to use their vote to enlarge government expenditures—since they would bear no part of the cost—and to place a larger burden on the remaining taxpayers. The resulting situation would be highly divisive. Advocates of using special tax provisions to "redistribute the tax burden" appear to forget that, in a democracy, tax institutions do more than influence the distribution of income; they are a cost-sharing device that has an effect on the size of government expenditures and on the cohesiveness of the community.

To say that it is desirable for the poor to pay taxes does not mean that we should ignore their plight. Use of government expenditure programs, with transfers unrelated to tax payments, can aid the poor without producing consequences like those of the tax credit. Consider a family receiving an NIT transfer payment unrelated to local tax payments. Would it irresponsibly vote for an increase in local government expenditures, to be financed by an increase in property taxes? Since the family would have to pay the higher property taxes itself, and since this would not increase the NIT transfer, it would be forced to weigh the benefits of greater government spending against its share of the costs.[35] If democratic political institutions are to function well, it is important that citizens share in the costs as well as the benefits of government policies. Manipulation of taxes to exempt people from any tax burden in the name of helping the poor is politically unwise. It is also unnecessary, since outright government expenditures can do the job of redistribution more effectively and more equitably.

Direct Intervention in Markets

One of the most common methods of attempting to aid the poor is to take direct action to influence the prices of the goods they buy or sell. High prices for the goods they sell will clearly benefit the poor, and minimum wage laws can ensure that no one is paid too low a wage. Low prices for the goods they purchase are desirable, and price ceilings, like rent controls, can keep prices down. Laws requiring "equal pay for equal work" and premium rates for overtime have similar goals. The government has shown little reluctance to interfere in the price-determining functions of markets, and a desire to help the poor is a major reason for policies of this type.

In contrast to the other policies examined, a basic characteristic of this type of policy is that it operates largely outside the government tax-expenditure process. The costs of administering market-intervention laws are quite modest relative to their impact. For that reason it is easy to overlook these alternatives in a discussion of welfare reform. But their potential impact on the distribution of income is enormous, so they should also be considered as policy options. Rather than discussing market intervention in general, I shall concentrate on one of the most politically entrenched of these policies, the minimum wage law. Following that discussion, the disadvantages of direct intervention in markets should be clear.

Minimum wage laws cause unemployment. When wage rates are set above market wage rates, employers can be expected to retrench by cutting back on the number of workers they employ.[36] This appears to be the reason why so many economists are opposed to minimum wage laws. But there are other side effects of the policy that are also undesirable. A floor under the wage rates that can be paid makes it very difficult for unskilled workers to receive on-the-job training. Generally, workers receive lower wages during training periods—in effect paying in that fashion for the training they receive. This becomes impossible for many workers when it is illegal for employers to pay a low wage rate. In addition, by creating a situation where there are more people desiring jobs than there are jobs available, minimum wage laws make it much less costly for employers to discriminate in their hiring practices. Since a surplus of qualified job applicants results, criteria other than productivity have to be used in determining who is to be employed.

These effects of minimum wage laws might be tolerable if the laws were an effective method of helping the poor. The main question is: who benefits and who loses? The main beneficiaries are those who remain employed at the minimum wage rate since they receive a higher wage. There is no doubt that many in this category are poor, but a great many are not. Working wives, youngsters in part-time jobs, college students in summer jobs, unmarried individuals (a single person working full time at a wage of only two-thirds the minimum wage will be above the poverty line)—people in these and other categories who are employed at the minimum wage rate are often not poor, but they receive a substantial share of the benefits of this law. A low wage rate for an individual worker simply does not imply a low family income. Others who benefit but are not poor include workers who are paid above the minimum but who compete with unskilled workers. This is the reason why it is in the interest of many labor unions to favor the law.

So the mandatory minimum wage rate does not concentrate its benefits on the poor. How does it distribute costs? The major losers are workers who cannot find jobs as a result of the law. Understandably, the least likely to find employment will be the least productive, most unskilled workers. A large portion of this group is certain to be poor in the absence of the law, and they are made even poorer as a result of it. Thus, the group we would normally want to help the most is hit the hardest by the law. Of course, members of the general public also bear a large share of the cost in the form of higher prices for products produced by industries using a large proportion of low-wage labor, and also in the form of lower wages for themselves. The way the higher labor costs are passed on through the system is not exactly known, since it depends on how all the various markets respond to the higher minimum rate. But in any case, it would be a coincidence if this part of the cost were shared in an equitable manner.

The distributional effects of minimum wage laws can be summarized simply: they are highly capricious. Many nonpoor are benefited and many poor are harmed. It is not necessary to argue over whether the amount of unemployment created is large to recognize the weakness of a minimum wage law as a program to help the poor. The arbitrary and capricious distribution of benefits and costs makes this redistribution technique very undesirable compared to policies capable of concentrating benefits on the poorest families and of allocating the costs fairly among the nonpoor.

All forms of direct intervention in markets share this defect to a large degree. The government can fix prices, but that power does not give it very effective control over the distribution of income. That fact, together with the dislocations caused by price fixing, probably accounts for the general preference among economists for transfers as a means of redistribution. I suspect that, of all the redistributive policies examined here, most economists would rank this type of policy lowest.

Fine Tuning the Welfare System?

Dozens of programs of the types reviewed in this chapter combine to form the welfare system in the United States. Having reviewed the separate parts of the system, it is now time to try to put the parts together and look at the system as a whole. Use of a multiplicity of programs can be viewed as an attempt to "fine tune" the welfare system. There are programs to cover most categories of poor people, to subsidize all of the most essential goods consumed, and to remove the causes of low incomes. There are laws designed to protect the poor from those who employ them and from those who sell to them. Finally some policies are intended to fill in the gaps left by other policies. Given the many goals to be achieved by the welfare system, a multifaceted approach seems entirely appropriate to many people.

Do the combined effects of these programs produce a sensible welfare system? It is certainly easy to imagine that the system as a whole would overcome the defects we noted in analyzing its individual parts. And it is true that the combined effects of the various programs are often quite different from what would appear from an examination of the separate programs. But it is the defects in the programs that are magnified by the interactions among them, not the strengths. Contradictions and anomalies pervade the present welfare system. To take a few examples:

(1) Job-training programs are supposed to augment the earning capacity of workers with limited skills. But it is quite possible that all the training provided by government does not offset the decline in on-the-job training produced as a result of the minimum wage law. Not only do those who are unemployed as a consequence of the law lose valuable experience and training, but also those who remain employed receive less training because it is not profitable for a firm to train unskilled workers if it cannot partially cover the costs by paying workers lower wages during the training period.

(2) Programs often interact to frustrate policy changes designed to help the poor. One might assume that an across-the-board increase in social security benefits would help the elderly poor. But for the elderly poor who are receiving SSI as well as social security, an increase in social security benefits is, in most cases, of no benefit at all. Higher social security payments reduce SSI payments, dollar for dollar, so a $100 increase under the former reduces benefits by $100 under the latter. Moreover, an elderly person receiving medicaid benefits may find that an increase in social security benefits makes him ineligible for medicaid altogether.

(3) Agricultural price supports (until recently), along with tariffs and quotas on agricultural products, work to increase the prices paid for food at the same time that food stamps (and the other food programs for the poor) are used to reduce food costs. For many families the benefits of food stamps are more than offset by the added costs imposed by these other programs.

(4) Restrictive labor-union practices (sanctioned by law), provisions of the Davis-Bacon Act, and minimum wage laws increase housing costs while another group of programs attempts to reduce them. A great many poor families, especially those not covered by present housing subsidies, are worse off because of this combination of policies.

(5) In attempting to offset the work-disincentive effects of high marginal tax rates in AFDC, the government requires work registration of some mothers. Work requirements are notoriously ineffective in the best of circumstances, but an unexpected reason for this ineffectiveness is afforded by the following example.[37] Suppose the penalty for refusal to work is a reduction in the AFDC monthly payment from $168 to $119, or by $49. The reduction in AFDC benefits, however, reduces the price the family must pay for food stamps and public housing, so the net cost of work refusal (due to the increased subsidies under the other programs) falls from $49 to $24. If there are any expenses associated with work, it is easy to see why this work requirement would be totally ineffective.

The list could be extended almost indefinitely, but the examples given suffice to make the point.

One claim that can indeed be made for the present system is that it redistributes an enormous volume of resources to those at the lower end of the income distribution. It is almost impossible, however, to determine how these benefits are divided among the low-income population. Due to the numerous programs that dispense benefits, the total transfer received by a family may depend on age and sex of the adults, presence or absence of an able-bodied male, age and sex of the children, employment status, occupation, duration of unemployment (if unemployed), and luck. Location is also very important, since benefits under AFDC, medicaid, and public housing vary substantially from state to state. Family income and size also play some role.

It is no surprise, then, that the combined benefits received by families show enormous variation. Typically, a family headed by an unemployed female could have received $5,312 in total benefits (equivalent to $5,890 in taxable income) in New York City in 1972, but the same family in Atlanta would have received only $2,710.[38] These figures include only cash assistance, food stamps, medicaid, and free school lunches. A very few families may do much better. A hypothetical compilation published in the *Congressional Record* reveals how a mother with four children in Portland, Oregon, could receive up to $13,799 in benefits (equivalent to a taxable income of $16,500) from a total of fifteen different programs.[39] At the other extreme, and no doubt much more common, is the male-headed family receiving nothing but food stamps.

The combined effects of programs often spell disaster for work incentives.[40] Not only are total benefits high for some families, implying a large income effect that is adverse to work, but also—and this is of even more importance—marginal tax rates are often exceedingly high. Consider a family receiving only food stamps. Under that program, earnings are taxed at rates of 25 to 30 percent. In addition, earnings are subject to a social security tax of about 12 percent (5.85 percent on the employee and 5.85 percent on the employer),[41] which raises the effective tax rate to 37 to 42 percent. Also, state income and sales taxes can be expected to add perhaps 3 percent, bringing the total to 40 to 45 percent.[42] This family would be able to keep only 62 cents of each dollar of earnings. And this 40 to 45 percent tax rate is effectively the *minimum* tax rate applied to welfare recipients since all low-income families are eligible for food stamps and all must pay social security taxes on any earnings from wages. For many poor families, the effective marginal tax rate is much larger.

Even though the implicit tax rate in each program may be quite low, when several programs simultaneously affect a family the *effective* marginal tax rate is approximately the sum of the separate rates. If the family described above lives in a public housing unit and pays 25 percent of its income in rent, its effective tax rate is about 65 to 70 percent. Families receiving benefits under AFDC face even higher marginal tax rates. Henry Aaron shows that a family receiving AFDC, food stamps, and housing assistance is subjected to a tax rate of nearly 80 percent beyond a very low level of earnings.[43] What the "typical" marginal tax rate is for families with low incomes is not known, but it must be well in excess of 40 percent. The present combination of welfare programs, then, does anything but avoid the work incentive problem that, to some extent, characterizes the NIT.

Problems like these cannot be avoided within the framework of the present welfare system (although they have been ameliorated in California by state reforms instituted in 1973). This system, according to a recent government publication, is composed of 168 different federal government expenditure programs which aid the poor[44] (not including special tax provisions or programs like the minimum wage law). These programs pass through about twenty different congressional committees and are administered by at least twelve different departments or agencies. Since many families receive benefits from several programs simultaneously, coordination is extremely important. It is clear that this large number of programs is not effectively coordinated at the present time. What is not clear is whether effective coordination is possible.

Not all of these 168 programs are equally important, of course. But at least 28 of them confer benefits to more than one million beneficiaries each. How prevalent the incidence of multiple benefits (families receiving benefits from two or more programs) is not known. A recent survey found that 20 percent of those who receive any benefits receive benefits from five or more programs.[45] The percentage of families receiving multiple benefits is certainly higher today, and growing.

The incredible complexity of the present welfare system imposes high costs on eligible families. "Poorly educated people are thrown up against a system that requires filling out multiple—and often unintelligible—forms to qualify for aid under the various programs."[46] In addition, they must plan their affairs with an eye toward making sure that they do not inadvertently become ineligible for a program dispensing important benefits. This means trying to understand the eligibility rules for a number of programs, rules that change frequently. The stereotype of the harried taxpayer arranging his affairs to take advantage of every "tax loophole" may soon be more appropriate to the harried welfare recipient.

Complexity also imposes costs on the well-intentioned reformer, whether he is a congressman or a concerned citizen. Constructive piecemeal change requires understanding the components of the system and how they interact. In order to be certain that a new program or a modification of an existing one will improve matters, it is necessary first to understand how the change will affect the 168 existing programs. Even a superficial understanding of the present system demonstrates how difficult it is to make small improvements.

A broad-based cash transfer program like the NIT is an attractive alternative to this melange of government programs. The NIT may compare poorly with some nonexistent welfare system that has no defects, but that description does not apply to the U.S. system. The case for the NIT is, to some degree, the case against the present system. Fine tuning the present system by using a multitude of separate programs has failed—understandably so, since it represents an attempt at government planning of an important part of a complex economic system, that part inhabited by the poor. While the NIT is no panacea, it is an effective mechanism for transferring money to the poor in a more equitable manner, at low administrative cost, and without the massive distortions that characterize the present system. Perhaps most important, it can be understood: by the recipients, the taxpayers, and the Congress.

CHAPTER IV

BROAD-BASED CASH TRANSFERS

The analysis in the last chapter made it easy to understand why the negative income tax is popular among economists. But the NIT is not without its own problems, and several of the more technical difficulties that arise in using this policy have not yet been discussed. (Space also has precluded an in-depth technical analysis of the many other redistribution policies covered in Chapter 3.)

This chapter presents a somewhat more detailed analysis of the NIT, as well as of two other, less well-known broad-based cash transfer programs. First, we shall examine each policy in isolation, ignoring the difficulties of coordinating it with a number of other programs. Then we shall look at the problems that arise when a broad-based cash transfer is simply added to the numerous policies already in existence.

The Negative Income Tax

Setting the Policy Variables. Ignoring for the moment the treatment of families of different sizes and the definition of income, an NIT plan can be described by its three policy variables: the income guarantee, the marginal tax rate, and the breakeven level of income. A simple graphical presentation is an even more convenient way to depict NIT plans. Figure 4-1 illustrates several alternative plans. In this figure, the horizontal axis measures pretransfer income, that is, the incomes of families before receiving transfers and the vertical axis measures disposable income, or pretransfer income plus any transfer. In the absence of any transfer program (or tax), pretransfer income and disposable income would be equal. This equality is shown by a 45 degree line, which has a slope of one, implying that

Figure 4-1

ILLUSTRATION OF ALTERNATIVE NIT PLANS

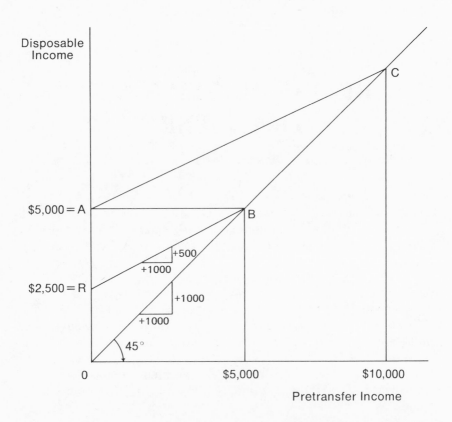

each additional $1,000 of pretransfer income adds exactly $1,000 to disposable income. (It should be noted that throughout this section four-member families are assumed.)

The NIT plan described in the last chapter had an income guarantee of $2,500, a marginal tax rate of 50 percent, and a breakeven income of $5,000 (a $2,500–50 percent NIT). This plan is shown in Figure 4-1 by the line RB. The transfer associated with each level of pretransfer income is equal to the vertical difference between RB and the no-transfer reference point, the 45 degree line. Thus, at a pretransfer income of zero, the transfer equals OR, or $2,500. The transfer is smaller at higher income levels (the distance between RB and the 45 degree line is smaller) until it reaches zero at $5,000, or at point B. An NIT, then, can be shown as a straight line, or transfer schedule, with the income guarantee given by the intercept with the horizontal axis (point R) and the breakeven income by the intercept with the 45 degree line (point B). The marginal tax rate is implied by the slope of the transfer schedule: it is equal to one minus the slope of the transfer schedule. Along RB, disposable income rises by $500 for each additional $1,000 in pretransfer income (because the transfer falls by $500), so the marginal tax rate is one-half.

Having illustrated an NIT plan graphically, let us turn now to the question of exactly where to set the policy variables. Consider the significance of each variable. The income guarantee is the transfer made to a family with a zero pretransfer income. Since this transfer will represent the entire disposable income of families with no other income, it is desirable that the income guarantee be high enough to permit a "decent" level of living. The marginal tax rate can have a major impact on work incentives. A high marginal tax rate reduces the incentive to earn because it means that disposable income rises very little when earnings increase. Thus, to preserve work incentives as much as possible, a low marginal tax rate is desirable. All families with incomes below the breakeven income will receive transfers. With a high breakeven income, not only will the cost of the plan be high because many families will be subsidized, but also there will be fewer families with incomes above the breakeven income to share the taxes necessary to finance the program. This suggests that a low breakeven income is desirable.

It appears advisable, then, to have a low breakeven income and a low tax rate, but a high income guarantee. Unfortunately, it is impossible to achieve simultaneously all these aims, because of the necessary relationship between the policy variables (with the income guarantee equal to the tax rate times the breakeven income). This is clearly shown in Figure 4-1. Suppose that the poverty line is $5,000 and that this figure is considered a reasonable income guarantee. If we choose to keep the breakeven income low—at $5,000, for example—the entire transfer schedule in the diagram is line AB. But this NIT involves a tax rate of 100 percent, because, as can be seen, disposable income does not rise with pretransfer income at all between zero and $5,000. So this plan would completely destroy all incentive to work: while it would restrict payments to those with incomes below the poverty line, it would be extremely costly since most recipients would have a strong incentive to stop contributing anything to their own support.

To maintain incentives it is essential that the marginal tax rate be well below 100 percent. There are two distinctly different ways to lower the marginal tax rate. One is to hold the income guarantee at $5,000 and lower the tax rate, but this implies a higher breakeven income. For example, a 50 percent tax rate and a $5,000 guarantee produces the transfer schedule shown by line AC, implying a break-even income of $10,000. This program would not completely destroy work incentives, but it would be very costly for it would involve transfers to more than 80 million persons. The other way to get a lower tax rate is to hold the breakeven income at $5,000 and lower the income guarantee. With a 50-percent tax rate we are then back at the schedule RB with a $2,500 income guarantee. This schedule would be even more conducive to work incentives than the program with an income guarantee of $5,000 and a 50-percent rate (line AC), but families with zero pretransfer income would have to make do on a disposable income of half the poverty level.

This discussion emphasizes the difficult, but inevitable, choices that must be made. A high guarantee with a high tax rate (implying a low breakeven income) restricts transfers to those with low incomes, but weakens work incentives greatly. On the other hand, a high guarantee with a low tax rate (implying a high breakeven income) involves a high cost which must be borne by the smaller number of families left above the breakeven income. This means that high tax rates must be applied to taxpayers, thereby weakening their incentives to work. A low guarantee with a moderate tax rate, like 50 percent, keeps costs manageable and retains some incentive to work, but the assistance given to families with the lowest incomes will then be modest.

Economics cannot resolve the question of what combination of policy variables is best. Ultimately that decision must reflect, to a degree, subjective values concerning the relative importance attached to the conflicting goals. All that economics can do is point out the necessity of making this choice. But it should be emphasized that this difficult choice is not unique to the NIT and cannot be avoided by using other types of policies. As we saw in the last chapter, many existing programs are in effect NITs restricted to certain categories of people or involving limitations on what may be consumed with the transfer. This means that the same difficult choices among policy variables must be made for these programs as well. Ultimately, the necessity of trading one desirable goal for another results from scarcity—that is, the condition of limited resources that makes it impossible to achieve all our wants simultaneously.

Probably the only general agreement among economists in this regard is the importance of keeping the marginal tax rate well below 100 percent. Many people, when first considering how to help people below the poverty line, think the best way is to give each family exactly enough to raise it to the poverty line, and not one dollar more. But this describes an NIT with a 100 percent marginal tax rate, like the transfer schedule AB in Figure 4-1, a schedule that would completely destroy all incentive for self-support. This arrangement is also inequitable in the view of many since it would mean that even if a family earned more than another before receiving a transfer, its after-transfer income would be no higher. Under the $5,000–100 percent NIT, a family earning a $4,000 pretransfer income would have the same disposable income as a family earning only $1,000.

Thus, if we are to have an income guarantee at all close to the poverty line, it is necessary—both for reasons of incentives and for considerations of fairness—to pay transfers to families above the poverty line. (That this seems anomalous to some people is probably yet another indication of how misleading it is to think of poverty in terms of a fixed poverty line and to see the implied goal as raising people to exactly that income level.) But this does not mean that a very large fraction of the total transfers paid will go to families with high incomes. For example, with the $5,000–50 percent NIT, which pays transfers up to its breakeven income of $10,000, I estimate that roughly 65 percent of the total payments would go to those who, before receiving transfers, have incomes below $5,000—assuming families do not reduce their present efforts to earn their own income. For a more moderate $4,000–50 percent NIT, about 75 percent of the transfers would go to families with pretransfer incomes below $5,000.[1] Of course, this means that many families with incomes initially below $5,000 would be raised not only to that level, but above it. However, as we have seen, that can hardly be avoided in a plan with a high minimum guarantee. In any event, the NIT is capable of concentrating most of its payments on those with low incomes. That is something that the current welfare system decidedly does not accomplish.

Work Incentives. In theory, an NIT program is expected to lead to a reduction in work effort. The income effect, resulting from the supplement to income (which makes it easier for a family to afford to work less), and the substitution effect, resulting from the marginal tax rate (which reduces the net rate of pay), both imply reduced work effort. It is not the tax rate alone that is important, then, but also the size of the transfer. A $3,000–50 percent NIT can be expected to reduce work effort more than a $2,000–50 percent NIT, although both use the same tax rate, because the income effect of the former program is larger.

Popular discussion of the work-incentive question generally emphasizes the importance of the income guarantee and suggests that to guarantee a person's income is to cause him or her to stop work altogether. But widespread idleness is not what economic theory predicts; rather it simply predicts a reduction in the number of hours of work per year. Working is not entirely an all-or-nothing matter. It is seriously misleading to depict the issue solely in terms of whether recipients will live exclusively "on the dole." Of course, some recipients may do exactly that, but economic theory alone does not permit us to determine how large an impact on work effort an NIT will have. Empirical research is required to estimate the magnitude of the work disincentive effect.

Before discussing the evidence that is available, we should try to explain why the work-incentive question is important. One reason is that the extent of the reduction in work effort has a major impact on the cost of the program. When earnings fall under a given NIT program, the transfer payments automatically rise and so do the costs to taxpayers. Roughly, each percentage point reduction in earnings increases the transfer payments by 1 percent.[2] Thus, if earnings are expected to fall by a third, then the cost of the program will increase by a third. This effect should be kept in mind in evaluating the cost estimates of various plans, because such estimates are generally based on the assumption of no change in earnings in response to the program.

A closely related reason is that the larger the disincentive effect the more difficult and more expensive it will be to increase the disposable incomes of low-income families. Suppose that under a $2,500–50 percent NIT a family initially earning $4,000 reduced its earnings to $3,000. It would then receive a transfer of $1,000 and have a post-transfer disposable income of $4,000, the same disposable income it had in the absence of the program. While such a response may be unlikely, it is by no means impossible, and the example illustrates that it could be very costly to increase the disposable incomes of recipients if the outcome were a substantial reduction in work effort. Note, however, that even in the extreme case where disposable income is not increased, the family would be better off: it would have the same money income but would have to work less to acquire it. But if the goal is to increase the consumption of goods *other than leisure* (goods like housing, medical care, clothing, and food), then this goal will be partially frustrated through a reduction in the recipients' work effort.

Another reason for concern about work effort is that the NIT induces an uneconomic substitution of leisure for work. Just as the food stamp program leads to overconsumption of food, the NIT leads to overconsumption of leisure. If the family described in the last paragraph were given $1,000 in cash regardless of its earnings, it would probably work more (since earnings would not be subject to, in effect, a 50 percent tax), and would be better off. Therefore, the NIT is not without distortions: it distorts the choice of how much to work. However, there is reason to believe that this distortion is of smaller magnitude than the distortions caused by other types of welfare programs.[3] It will be recalled that the food stamp program not only affects work incentives (as does the NIT), but it also distorts how the family spends its remaining disposable income.

A final reason is purely paternalistic. The view seems to be widely held that work is important in giving meaning to life and in producing a sense of fulfillment and self-respect. To the extent that low-income families share this view of the importance of the work ethic, and there is some evidence that they do, this would lessen the reduction in work that an NIT would produce.

The empirical evidence bearing on the question of work incentives is of two general types: (1) studies of the actual reactions of low-income families to different wage rates and existing welfare programs like AFDC and social security (programs that are similar in relevant respects to the NIT) and (2) studies of the results of an experimental NIT program conducted between 1968 and 1971 which covered several hundred families in New Jersey and Pennsylvania.[4] The results of this experiment have recently become available.

In surveying the non-experimental evidence, Irwin Garfinkel points out that while the data support the view that work effort will be reduced in response to an NIT, there is still wide disagreement about exactly how large the reduction would be.[5] For example, among prime-aged married men, the estimated reduction in work effort for a $3,000–50 percent NIT (family of four) ranges from 3 percent to 40 percent. According to Garfinkel, the studies yielding the largest estimates contain severe technical problems. But even if this group of studies is discounted, we are left with a wide range of uncertainty. The reason is that it is extremely difficult to identify what causes some families to work less than others.

One conclusion that Garfinkel draws from the studies of existing programs is that work-effort response tends to vary among demographic groups. The evidence suggests that prime-aged married men will reduce work effort less than will prime-aged married women, prime-aged women who are heads of families, and older men. Apparently, persons in these last three groups are more responsive to a stimulus inducing less work. This is an interesting finding because two of these three groups, that is, older men and female heads of families, are covered by existing welfare programs—social security and old age assistance (now SSI) for older men and AFDC for female-headed families. Sometimes these programs are defended on the grounds that elderly men and female heads of families are not very responsive to financial incentives to work, but the evidence points to greater reductions in work effort for these groups than for prime-aged married men. However, the lower reductions estimated for prime-aged married men may simply reflect our inability to estimate the effects for a group that has not, until quite recently (with food stamps), been granted any sizeable transfers.

The New Jersey and Pennsylvania NIT experiment has yielded direct information for prime-aged married men and women.[6] On average, hours worked fell by 6 percent for men and 15 percent for women.[7] However, for a number of reasons, this body of evidence is also far from conclusive. First, the duration of the experiment was limited. The participating families knew that payments would end after three years, and this may have led them to respond differently than they would have under a permanent program. Second, the families not receiving transfers (the control group that provided the basis for estimating what the participating families would have done in the absence of the program) were, however, eligible for and sometimes receiving benefits under existing welfare programs in New Jersey and Pennsylvania. Perhaps the control group was induced to work less because of these programs and, if so, the estimated impact on the work effort of the experimental group would be too low.

A final difficulty with the experiment is that, of necessity, it covered only a small fraction of those who would be covered by a national program. The responses of participants in any such experiment may be quite different from the responses generated by a national program which would involve all low-income families. To give one illustration of why this might be so, consider a person in the experiment who wished to work thirty hours a week instead of forty. It is unlikely that an employer would permit only one of his employees to work a short week, so the participant in the NIT experiment would either have to work forty hours or quit. He would probably decide to continue working since, after the experiment ended, he would presumably want to continue at forty hours a week. In this case, the experiment would not produce a reduction in work effort. But a reduction would occur under the same NIT if the program were permanent and had universal coverage. In a permanent nationwide program, many workers would want a shortened work week, and employers would have a strong incentive to accommodate this desire since if they did not, they would lose workers to other employers who were more responsive to their workers' wishes.[8]

While it is clear that the available evidence does not permit a precise estimate of the impact of any specific NIT on work effort, two general conclusions can be drawn. First, the economists' emphasis on work incentives has not been misplaced. People do respond to monetary incentives. To the extent that our inadequate knowledge permits, that fact should be taken into account in the design of the program. Second, the fear that there might be complete cessation of work appears to be exaggerated. The evidence suggests that there would be a reduction in hours worked, but complete withdrawal from the labor force, especially for prime-aged married men, would be unlikely on a significant scale.

It should be emphasized that the estimates of reduced work effort given in this section are based on a comparison of work disincentives under an NIT and under no welfare program at all. But recall that existing programs already contain substantial work disincentives. Replacing these programs with a well-designed NIT might not reduce work effort any further and, indeed, might even improve the situation.

The Definition of Income. The importance of the definition of income used for the purpose of computing the NIT transfer can be illustrated by a few examples. If the definition is the one currently employed in the federal individual income tax law, interest on state and local government bonds would not be included because this interest is not treated as income under present law. Thus if a family had interest income of $10,000 from this source and no other income, it would be entitled to receive the income guarantee of the NIT. Or consider a farming family with money income of $2,000. If that family also raised $1,000 worth of food crops for home consumption, it would receive the same transfer as a city family with $2,000 in earnings but only the food that it purchased in the market.

These examples illustrate how a narrow definition of income can lead to inequities. For NIT purposes it is desirable that income be defined in such a way that a low income corresponds to economic need. If it is not, many families who are not really needy could receive transfers. Therefore, what is required is a broad definition of income, one that includes "all income from whatever source derived" (in the words of the Internal Revenue Code). The many practical difficulties of implementing that general principle are well recognized, and they need not be stressed here since the same issues are involved in defining taxable income under the federal individual income tax.[9]

More than equity is at issue in the definition of taxable income. The exclusion of certain items from the definition can create strong economic incentives to convert ordinary income into kinds of income exempt from taxation. Suppose we have a $3,000–50 percent NIT, with all food expenditures deductible from income to arrive at "taxable" income. A family with earnings of $3,000 that spends $1,000 on food will then receive a transfer of $2,000, instead of the $1,500 it would get if the full $3,000 in earnings counted as income. The extra $500 transfer means that the government is, in effect, paying half of the family's food cost. This would be true whatever the amount of food purchased: for every additional dollar's worth of food, taxable income would fall by a dollar and the transfer would increase by fifty cents. Thus, the effect of this deduction, or "tax loophole," would be to reduce the price of food to transfer recipients by 50 percent, to induce them to consume more food, and to increase the cost of the NIT. It would also lead to overconsumption of food, just as the food stamp program does. In general, recipients would be better off under a plan with a higher income guarantee and with larger transfer payments they could spend as they chose.

Showing how NIT "tax loopholes" work to subsidize consumption of particular items points up once again the importance of the marginal tax rate. If the loophole is special treatment of food expenditures and if the tax rate is 67 percent, for instance, a dollar spent on food increases the transfer by 67 cents, so the net price of food to recipients would be only a third of the market price of food. The higher the marginal tax rate, the greater the subsidy given to consumption of items deductible from income. But, as we have seen, a reasonably low marginal tax rate is important not only to limit work disincentives but also to avoid too strong an inducement to convert income into nontaxable forms. However, in order to keep the cost of an NIT program within bounds, the marginal tax rate will probably have to be fairly high—close to 50 percent, if not higher. This makes the problems of tax loopholes more acute in the NIT than in the federal income tax: very few federal taxpayers are in a marginal tax bracket of 50 percent or above, but it is probable that all transfer recipients would be.

Tax loopholes would increase the NIT's flexibility as a transfer program. If it is considered desirable to encourage consumption of particular items, allowing expenditures on those items to be deducted from income would be an effective way to achieve that goal.

For instance, allowing NIT participants to deduct the cost of health insurance premiums would encourage them to purchase this kind of insurance and would be an attractive alternative to a national health insurance program. However, for reasons discussed in Chapter 3, the economic case for using what amounts to a form of in-kind transfer is not particularly strong, and the political dangers of abusing this policy tool are obviously great.

Incentive to Invest in Human Capital. One frequently ignored aspect of the NIT is its possible impact on incentives to invest in human capital, that is, to increase one's earning capacity. Consider again a $3,000–50 percent NIT plan. If a participant in that plan is earning $4,000 (and receiving a transfer of $1,000), and if he has the opportunity to take training that will enable him to earn $6,000, how much would this investment be worth to him? Increasing his earning potential from $4,000 to $6,000 will not increase his annual net income by $2,000, since the transfer payment would fall to zero if his income increased to $6,000. The net increment in income is only $1,000 (the $2,000 gross increase minus the reduction in the transfer payment). Thus, a 50-percent marginal tax rate cuts in half the return to be obtained from increasing one's earning capacity.

One mitigating factor in the NIT is that it would make it easier for recipients to afford job training. The person who stops working to undertake training receives the basic income guarantee—which can help defray the costs of the training. This may partially offset the reduced returns available, but it is unlikely to offset them fully, especially if the tax rate is very high. For example, suppose the NIT tax rate is 100 percent. In this case, an increase in earning potential does not increase net income at all (unless it raises earnings above the breakeven level of income), and there can be little doubt that job training will be quite unattractive investments for welfare recipients.

Once again, the significance of the marginal tax rate is apparent. In the short run, work incentives may be impaired by a high marginal tax rate and, in the long run, work skills may be allowed to deteriorate or may never be acquired in the first place. The significance of this latter effect extends far beyond training programs, narrowly conceived. Among other things, public schools are a type of generalized job training for children. For children with little ambition or ability, the advantage in terms of higher future incomes from doing well in school would be significantly reduced by an NIT program with a high marginal tax rate.

Treatment of the Family Unit. That transfers should be related to family size as well as family income is obvious. A $2,000 transfer may be adequate for a single individual but would hardly sustain life for a family of six with no other income. However, there are some difficult choices to be made in deciding exactly how to treat families of different sizes.

Table 4-1 gives three alternative NIT plans which differ in their treatment of families of different size. Plan A varies the guarantee in approximately the same way as do the official poverty lines, that is, the guarantee for a single individual equals half the guarantee for a family of four. Plan B is based on an equal per capita guarantee, $1,000 per person regardless of family size. Plan C involves a per capita guarantee of $1,200 for each adult and $800 for each child. All three plans provide an income guarantee of $4,000 for a family of four (composed of two adults and two children), and the costs of the three plans would probably be about the same.

There are three basic goals to be considered in deciding how to treat families of different sizes: (1) equity, or ensuring that the transfer reflects the different costs of supporting alternative sized families, (2) avoiding incentives to increase family size in order to increase the transfer payment, and (3) avoiding incentives to split larger families into smaller units. Unfortunately, these goals conflict, and it is not possible to achieve all three simultaneously.

Consider first the effect on family size. Since it costs more to support a larger family than a smaller one, equity calls for larger transfers to larger families, and all three plans in Table 4-1 embody

---

Table 4-1

ILLUSTRATION OF ALTERNATE INCOME GUARANTEES,
BY FAMILY SIZE AND COMPOSITION

Family Size and Composition	Plan A	Plan B	Plan C
1 (1 adult)	$2,000	$1,000	$1,200
2 (1 adult, 1 child)	2,600	2,000	2,000
2 (2 adults)	2,600	2,000	2,400
3 (1 adult, 2 children)	3,250	3,000	2,800
3 (2 adults, 1 child)	3,250	3,000	3,200
4 (2 adults, 2 children)	4,000	4,000	4,000
5 (2 adults, 3 children)	4,500	5,000	4,800
6 (2 adults, 4 children)	5,000	6,000	5,600

this characteristic. But this means that a family can increase its transfer by having more children. Under Plan A, if family size is increased from three to four, the transfer increases by $750. This "bonus" for additional children exists for all families whose incomes are below the breakeven level. Thus, assuming Plan A uses a 50-percent marginal tax rate, a family of three receives no transfer if its pretransfer income is $6,500 (the breakeven level for a three-person family), but would receive $750 if it had a second child since the breakeven income for a family of four is $8,000. Of course, this incentive could be avoided by providing the same guarantee for families of all sizes, but that would produce hardship for large families and a bonanza for small ones.

This same incentive is present in the federal income tax law, but it is of much smaller magnitude. A personal exemption of $750 is allowed to taxpayers, but the net gain in tax savings is much smaller than that. For a family with an income of $10,000 and a 20 percent marginal tax rate, taxes fall by $150 (20 percent of $750) when an extra family member is added, which represents a net increase in income of less than 2 percent. By contrast, a $750 net increase in income for a low-income family represents a sizeable percentage increase in income, perhaps large enough to affect decisions about family size.

The conflict between equity and avoiding incentives to increase family size is clear. Now consider the possible impact of transfer payments on family structure. Under Plan A, a family of four with no income receives $4,000. But if the husband leaves the wife and children (or appears to leave them), he receives $2,000, the guarantee for a single individual, and they receive $3,250. By splitting up, the total transfer is increased from $4,000 to $5,250. Similarly, two single individuals qualify for a transfer of $2,000 each, or $4,000, but if they marry their combined transfer falls to $2,600. Of course, there are extra costs in maintaining separate households, and this factor should mitigate the incentive to split up the family.

Plan B and Plan C produce no incentives to split larger family units into smaller ones, since a given number of people receives the same total transfer regardless of how many separate family units are involved. However, in both plans the guarantee for a single individual is far below the poverty line. This cannot be avoided if the per capita guarantees are set so that they produce a guarantee for a family of four equal to the poverty line. In addition, these plans provide guarantees above the poverty line for families larger than four, ignoring the economies of scale achievable in supporting larger families.

The conflict between equity and incentives necessitates a compromise. If decisions about family size and structure were unaffected by financial considerations, the choice would be easy. We would then choose Plan A which takes into consideration the different per capita costs for families of varying sizes. But experience under AFDC suggests that decisions about family size and structures are influenced by the pecuniary incentives built into the program. If the impact of pecuniary incentives is small, we could still lean towards Plan A. But it is not known exactly how responsive families are to these incentives. Most people have concluded that a program like Plan C is the best compromise, even though this type of plan creates incentives to have children in order to increase the transfer received and also makes a transfer to a single individual that is well below his poverty line.[10]

Coordination with the Federal Individual Income Tax. If the breakeven income of an NIT exceeds the sum of exemptions and deductions under the federal income tax, there will be a problem of coordinating the NIT and the positive income tax. Figure 4-2 illustrates this case. Under current federal income tax provisions, a family of four with an income above $4,300 pays taxes. (The $4,300 figure is the sum of $3,000 in personal exemptions and a $1,300 deduction for the low-income allowance.)[11] In the absence of the NIT, the relationship between pretransfer income and disposable income is given by the line OMD: over the MD range—above $4,300 in pretransfer income—disposable income is lower than pretransfer income because of the income taxes paid.

Now let us add a $3,000–50 percent NIT program, implying a breakeven income of $6,000. Since families in the income range from $4,300 to $6,000 pay federal income taxes, it is necessary to coordinate the NIT and the income tax in some way. One way would be to leave the present income tax law unchanged. Then families in the $4,300 to $6,000 range would simultaneously pay income taxes and receive NIT transfers. Their effective marginal tax rate would then be very high, since an additional dollar in earnings would not only reduce the NIT transfer but also increase federal tax liability. The tax and transfer together would produce a combined marginal tax rate of 64 or 65 percent (50 percent under the NIT plus 14 or 15 percent under the income tax, depending on the exact level of income). Nor is that all. Since these families would also be paying social security taxes and state income taxes, their effective tax rates under all programs combined would probably exceed 75 percent— much too high a figure to preserve incentives.

Figure 4-2

COORDINATION OF A $3,000–50 PERCENT NIT WITH
THE FEDERAL INCOME TAX

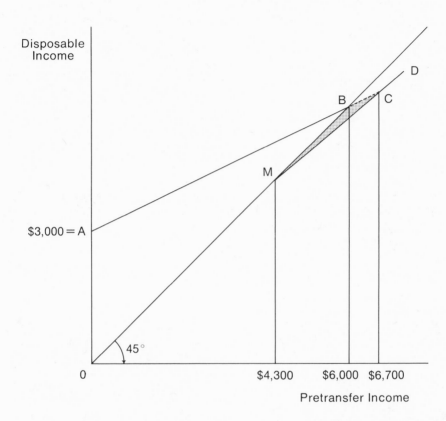

An alternative method of coordination would be to exempt
families in the $4,300 to $6,000 range from income taxes altogether,
but to require families with incomes above $6,000 to pay income
taxes according to present tax law. This would mean that a family
with $6,000 in pretransfer income would pay no tax (and receive
no transfer), but if it earned $1.00 more, its federal tax liability would
be $245 (since this is the tax liability under present law for an income
of $6,001) and its net income would fall. In effect, this method of
coordination involves a marginal tax rate far in excess of 100 percent
on earnings just above $6,000. That is clearly undesirable.

A third method of coordination, and the one most people prefer
to the other two, is to exempt families in the $4,300 to $6,700 range
from the income tax and apply the 50 percent rate of the NIT to
income in excess of $6,000, up to $6,700. This makes the effective

relationship between pretransfer income and disposable income equal to ABCD in Figure 4-2. The significance of the $6,700 figure is that the tax liability under this method of coordination is $350 at $6,700 (equal to 50 percent of the excess over $6,000), and this is the tax liability under present income tax provisions for an income of $6,700. In other words, this method simply extends the NIT transfer schedule, AB, in a straight line until it intersects the federal income tax schedule at point C, or $6,700. This means that the effective marginal tax rate for all families below $6,700 will be 50 percent (ignoring other taxes like the social security tax), but will drop to 15 percent just above $6,700 according to present income tax provisions.

There is little doubt that this method of coordination, or something very much like it, should be used. As a consequence, however, the NIT program will redistribute income in favor of families above its breakeven level in the form of reduced federal income tax liabilities. The shaded area in Figure 4-2 shows the reductions in tax liabilities. All families with incomes below the $6,700 level, which is sometimes called the tax breakeven level, will receive a net transfer in the form of either an explicit transfer or a tax reduction or (over the $4,300–$6,000 range) both.

All of our earlier analysis concerning the effects of high marginal tax rates applies to income levels above the breakeven income up to the tax breakeven income. Work incentives, for example, can be expected to be affected for families that are not receiving transfers—in the $6,000 to $6,700 range. And for larger NIT programs, the range of income above the breakeven income where these effects can be expected to occur will be even greater. For a $4,000–50 percent NIT with a breakeven income of $8,000, the tax breakeven income is about $10,000, so families in the $8,000 to $10,000 range will be subjected to marginal tax rates of 50 percent. And for a $5,000–50 percent NIT, the tax breakeven income is about $12,500, or $2,500 above the breakeven income of the plan.

Whether the NIT has an effect on families above the tax breakeven income depends on how it is financed. If financed entirely by reducing other transfers to low-income families, then the federal income tax rates above $6,700 in Figure 4-2 need not be increased. Other expenditures must be cut to finance the NIT transfers as well as the reductions in taxes shown by the shaded area in the diagram if higher taxes above $6,700 are to be avoided. If other expenditures are not cut, or are not cut sufficiently to fully finance the NIT then tax rates or incomes above $6,700 must be increased to finance the additional redistribution.

The NIT Relative to Alternative Programs. A closer look at the NIT reveals that it has some real drawbacks and poses some hard choices. However, it must be stressed that these problems are not unique to the NIT. Problems regarding selection of the policy variables, the definition of income, treatment of the family unit, and so on exist for most of the alternative policies discussed in Chapter 3 as well as for the NIT. In those few cases where a specific problem of the NIT can be avoided by using a different policy, that policy usually involves even worse problems of its own. So the case for the NIT as an alternative to other policies is not weakened by recognizing that it is no panacea. Rather, the disadvantages emphasized in this chapter are typical of those encountered in any type of redistribution policy. In this regard, one advantage of the NIT is that it is easy to understand the necessity of compromising among conflicting goals, so the final hard choices *that must be made* are more likely to be solidly based on a consideration of the factors involved.

Demogrants

Demogrants are a different form of broad-based cash transfer. A demogrant is an equal cash transfer made to all members of a demographic group, regardless of income. Most frequently the proposal is intended to apply to all citizens. Thus, a program involving a $1,000 annual transfer to every man, woman, and child would be a universal demogrant. (In the past, this policy was usually referred to as a "social dividend plan.")

The demogrant approach might appear to avoid one of the main defects of the NIT. Since every family of four receives, for example, the same $4,000 payment from the government regardless of its own income, the demogrant does not involve an explicit marginal tax rate which, in the NIT, reduces transfers for families with higher incomes. Therefore, the work incentive and other problems associated with the NIT's marginal tax rate seem to be avoided. Actually, this appearance is illusory because demogrants are basically a form of the NIT.

If a payment of $1,000 is made to every man, woman, and child, then the total outlay on this program would be about $210 billion— since the U.S. population is about 210 million. Somewhere $210 billion in taxes must be found to finance these outlays, and therein lies the rub. Almost the only tax base large enough to finance this sum is total income of all families—without exemptions or deductions. Even using this tax base, which is larger than any currently being

Figure 4-3

HYPOTHETICAL DEMOGRANT PROGRAM FINANCED BY A FLAT RATE TAX ON INCOME

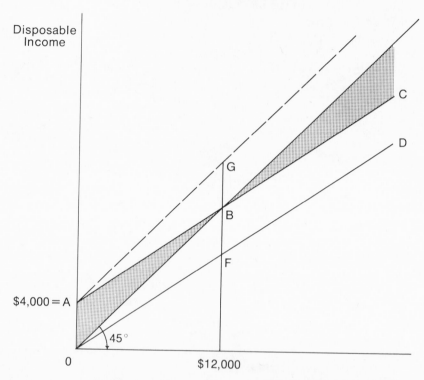

used, a flat rate income tax of approximately 33 percent would be required to finance this program alone. Since all income would be subject to tax, poor and nonpoor families would find their disposable income increasing only by 67 cents when an extra dollar was earned (and this ignores taxes required to finance other programs). Thus, this demogrant has the same effect on low-income families as a $4,000–33 percent NIT.

The equivalence between demogrants and the NIT can be seen most easily with the aid of Figure 4-3. The effect of the transfer payments alone is shown by the dotted line which is parallel to the 45 degree line and lies $4,000 above it. Income taxes to finance these payments are shown by the tax schedule OD which has a slope of two-thirds, implying a tax rate of one-third. The net effect of the tax and transfer policies is determined by subtracting the tax payment from the $4,000 transfer at each income level. This yields the net schedule ABC, which relates the combined tax and transfer effects on disposable income at all levels. It is clear that this demogrant simply redistributes income from families with income above $12,000 to those below, and the net effect is identical to a $4,000–33 percent NIT financed with a flat rate tax of one-third on income above the breakeven level. The diagram, of course, ignores the existence of other taxes and transfers in the system. When these are taken into account, the effective marginal tax rates would be well above 33 percent.

There are some superficial differences between this type of universal demogrant and the NIT. One is that this proposal involves the same marginal tax rate on everyone, recipients and taxpayers alike. This, however, could be avoided by using a graduated rate structure in the income tax. Another difference is that the demogrant program is likely to be more confusing to the public, since it is more difficult to figure out exactly who is benefiting and who is bearing the costs. Milton Friedman has stressed this point.[12] Indeed, it would be nearly impossible to determine the exact distributional effects if the program were financed not with a flat-rate tax on income, but instead with a combination of excise, corporate income, payroll, and other taxes.

These differences should not obscure the point that demogrants are fundamentally a variation on the NIT. All of our analysis of the NIT applies equally well to demogrants, so there is no need to repeat that analysis here. In fact, it is surprising how many apparently dissimilar programs to redistribute income are simply variations on the basic NIT theme. This point was implied in the last chapter, where we saw how many existing programs are just NIT plans with special wrinkles, and it is equally true for many of the proposed policies.

For our purposes the demogrant has one significant advantage: it requires only simple arithmetic to determine the tax rates applied to both taxpayers and transfer recipients. We shall make use of that advantage in the next chapter when we try to determine how much redistribution a society can afford.

Wage-Rate Subsidies

The potentialities of subsidizing wage rates rather than annual income have attracted the attention of a number of economists.[13] Less widely understood than the NIT, wage-rate subsidies constitute one of the few fundamentally different approaches to redistribution.

Under a wage-rate subsidy (WRS), recipients would receive cash transfers from the government, just as they do with the NIT. However, the size of the transfer would not be related to total pretransfer income, but instead would depend on wage rates and hours worked in such a way that recipients would receive a larger total transfer by working more.

Table 4-2 illustrates how a hypothetical WRS plan would work. In effect, the government would supplement low market wage rates. If a worker is paid $1.00 an hour by his employer, the government adds a subsidy of $1.00 per hour, so the net wage rate (including the subsidy) becomes $2.00 per hour. At higher wage rates the subsidy is reduced, but not by the full amount of the increment in the market wage rate. This is important because the net wage rate must always be higher when the market wage rate is higher: if this were not true workers would have no incentive to find jobs where their market wage rates (and hence productivities) are as high as possible. At a market wage rate of $3.00 the subsidy is zero, so the market and net wage rates are equal. The wage rate at which the subsidy is zero can be called the breakeven wage rate. A WRS program can be described by its breakeven wage rate and the rate of subsidy it embodies. The rate of subsidy determines how large the subsidy will be for market wage rates below the breakeven wage rate. For the WRS in Table 4-2, the rate of subsidy is one-half, which means that the subsidy is one-half the difference between the breakeven wage rate and the market wage rate. For instance, at a market wage rate of $2.00, the subsidy is equal to one-half of ($3.00 − $2.00), or $.50 per hour.

The total transfer payment received per year under a WRS depends on both the worker's wage rate and how many hours he works. At a market wage rate of $1.00, employment for 1,000 hours per year yields a total transfer of $1,000, while employment for

---

Table 4-2
HYPOTHETICAL WAGE-RATE SUBSIDY PLAN

Market Wage Rate	Subsidy	Net Wage Rate
$1.00	$1.00	$2.00
1.50	.75	2.25
2.00	.50	2.50
2.50	.25	2.75
3.00	0	3.00

2,000 hours a year yields a transfer of $2,000. Thus, the more work done the larger the total transfer, which is exactly the opposite of the situation under the NIT.

Advantages of the WRS. The principal advantage of the WRS is its impact on work incentives. Under this program, workers can get larger government transfers by working more. There is no incentive to stop work at all, since the transfer would be zero for workers who do not work. A WRS provides no income guarantee, and so problems related to that aspect of the NIT are avoided.

It does not follow, however, that recipients of WRS transfers will increase their work effort. A WRS affects a worker in exactly the same way as a wage-rate increase. Economic theory suggests that a higher wage rate may lead a worker to either increase or reduce his work effort, depending on his particular preferences for leisure relative to money income. The reason for this indefinite conclusion can be seen by considering the income and substitution effects of a higher wage rate. A higher wage rate implies a larger money income for the same amount of work, and this means that the worker does not have to work so hard to support himself: he can work fewer hours and earn the same income he got before the wage-rate increase. This is the income effect, and it favors less work. But a higher wage rate also has a substitution effect favorable to more work. At a higher wage rate the worker sacrifices more money if he reduces his work effort—which means, simply, that it is more expensive in terms of foregone earnings to consume leisure. The substitution effect favors more work, because work is now more highly remunerated. Since the substitution and income effects have opposing effects on work effort, the net effect of the two is theoretically unpredictable. In all likelihood, some workers would work more and some less. Empirical evidence, though not conclusive, seems to suggest that higher wage rates have only a small effect on average hours of work.[14]

One frequently mentioned objection to a WRS is that employers would reduce market wage rates in response to a WRS, thereby dissipating the gain to workers. This concern is largely unfounded. Competition among employers for the labor services of WRS recipients would bid market wage rates up to a level corresponding to the economic productivity of the workers. If one employer should try to lower his wage rates, his lower-paid workers would become a good bargain to other employers who would bid among themselves to hire these workers. The bidding would continue until the market wage rate of workers was equal to their productivity. A WRS would not interfere with this process and would not affect worker productivity, so market wage rates would not be directly affected by the program.

Market wage rates might be indirectly affected, however. If a WRS increased labor supply, this larger supply of labor would push down market wage rates. In this case, it would not be the WRS per se, but the larger number of workers seeking jobs, that depressed wages. As shown above, it is not clear whether there would be an increase in supply. If there were, workers would still be better off, since a larger number of workers would be attracted into the market only if the net wage rate (including the WRS subsidy) were above the preexisting market wage rate. But effects on market wage rates would be likely to be small, since the labor supply is not highly responsive to changes in wage rates. Hence the possibility of changes in market wage rates induced by changes in total labor supply will be ignored in this discussion. However, all of the conclusions stated here can be shown to hold in the cases where market conditions would produce a change in market wage rates.[15]

Since a WRS may either increase or reduce work effort, how can we speak of its work incentive effect as one of its advantages? The answer is that the WRS produces greater work incentives than other transfer programs. The comparison above was between a WRS and no transfer program at all. However, for the purpose of choosing among alternative transfer programs, this is not the relevant comparison. Instead, we should compare work effort under a WRS and, say, an NIT. When this comparison is made, it is clear that a WRS would lead to greater work effort than an NIT.

Let us consider transfers of the same amount of money to a person under these two alternative arrangements. Since the amounts are the same, the income effects of the transfers are identical: both raise the worker's earnings by the same amount. Therefore, it is the *substitution* effects of the two programs which will determine any difference in the net outcome. Since the substitution effect of the NIT discourages work and that of the WRS encourages work, work effort will be greater under the WRS. Thus, the work incentive effect of a WRS is superior to that of an NIT even though a WRS may or may not lead to greater work effort than no transfer program at all.

This conclusion should not be particularly surprising. After all, the NIT is basically a subsidy to leisure, since more leisure (less work) means a larger transfer, while the WRS is a subsidy to work. Given the importance of the work incentives issue, this conclusion is important. It means that, at a given cost to taxpayers, the WRS would lead to greater total money income for recipients than would the NIT. Put differently, the cost to taxpayers of increasing the money income of recipients by $X billion would be lower under the WRS, because the recipients would earn more income on their own.

A higher *money* income for recipients under the WRS does not necessarily mean that they would be better off than with an equivalent NIT. They would have higher incomes, but they would work more hours and so have less leisure time. They would have more of one desirable good—money—but less of another—leisure. There is no way to determine whether the recipients would prefer this outcome to that of the NIT without knowing the relative values they place on leisure and money. Whether taxpayers would prefer the WRS over the NIT depends on what they consider the goal of the redistribution to be. If the goal is to increase the money in the hands of the recipients, then the WRS would be preferred. Of course, money is simply a means of increasing the recipients' consumption of real goods—housing, clothing, food, and so on. Since concern about poverty is usually expressed in terms of money incomes (as in the official poverty lines) or consumption of essential goods, it appears that most taxpayers care less about the leisure consumed by the poor than about the disposable incomes of the poor (including in-kind income). If so, taxpayers would prefer the WRS because of its work incentive effect. However, there are other factors to be considered before any final judgment about the WRS and the NIT can be made.

Without doubt, the work incentive effect of the WRS is its main advantage. It has several less important advantages. For instance, it applies bigger subsidies to those with lower market wage rates, which is roughly in accord with accepted notions of fairness. In addition, it might be somewhat easier to integrate into the present system of transfer programs than the NIT, as we shall see later.

Disadvantages of the WRS. Compared to the NIT, the WRS has a number of disadvantages. One is that the WRS may not concentrate benefits on the poorest families. As noted in connection with minimum wage law, low wage rates do not necessarily imply low family incomes. Yet a WRS policy of the type outlined in Table 4-2 would benefit anyone working at a low wage rate. For example, if a husband works at $3.00 an hour and his wife at $2.00 an hour, and if both work full time, their combined annual income is $10,000—well above the poverty lines. But under the WRS the wife would receive a transfer of $1,000 per year (2,000 hours times the subsidy of $.50 per hour). Teenagers working part-time at low wages would also be subsidized, regardless of their parents' incomes.[16]

This difficulty with the WRS can perhaps be partially avoided by restricting the subsidy to the head of the family. However, this could lead to other problems. It would create incentives for husbands and wives to separate so that both could qualify as a family head. In addition, when several members of a family work, who is to be specified as the family head? If the choice is left up to the family, the member with the lowest wage rate would logically be selected since he or she would receive the largest subsidy. That would lead to many decidedly nonpoor families receiving transfers.

In its pure form the WRS takes no account of family size. A person earning $2.00 an hour would get the same hourly subsidy whether he supports only himself or a family of six. This suggests that it may be desirable to have the breakeven wage rate, and hence the subsidy per hour, depend on the size of the family. That modification would make the WRS more like the NIT where transfers depend on family size as well as on income. However, adjusting the WRS to take account of family size introduces the same incentives to alter family size and composition that we found with the NIT.

Another sticky problem of the same type is what to do about nonwage income. Many families have income from sources other than wages. An elderly person may have a pension, for example, and work to supplement his income. If no account is taken of the pension, he might receive a wage-rate subsidy even though his total income were well above the poverty line. There is no obviously satisfactory way to make adjustments for nonwage income.

All of the above problems relate to the inability of the WRS to confine benefits to people regarded as poor. They derive ultimately from the fact that poverty is generally defined in terms of the family unit and total money income from all sources. If this is the appropriate way to regard poverty, then it is doubtful that any WRS can target its benefits as accurately as the NIT. Adjustments made to mitigate these shortcomings would produce a more complicated WRS bound to have other unintended side effects.

A second disadvantage of the WRS is its effect on the incentive to invest in human capital. It is useful to distinguish two ways in which a worker can increase his earnings. One is to work longer hours at a given wage rate, and the WRS encourages this behavior. A second is to increase his wage rate, either through training to increase productivity or through a more careful search to find the job best suited to his abilities. The WRS discourages this second method of increasing earnings. Using the figures in Table 4-2, if a worker increases his market wage rate from $2.00 to $2.50, his net wage rate increases by only $.25 since the subsidy per hour falls to $.25. This leads to a smaller incentive to augment earning capacity. The NIT, however, has this same effect, so this does not provide a basis for favoring the NIT over the WRS.

The effect a WRS would have on the incentive to seek a higher market wage rate depends on the rate of subsidy used in the program. If the subsidy rate were one, implying that all low wage rates are supplemented to bring them up to $3.00, then no gain results from a higher market wage rate. In addition, if a worker's net wage rate is $3.00 regardless of his market wage rate, he would have no incentive to work in a job where his skills are most valuable: it would make no difference to his net wage rate whether his market rate was $1.00 or $2.50. This would severely impair the functioning of labor markets as they allocate people among jobs. To avoid this problem, it is important to keep the rate of subsidy in the WRS well below one. A rate of subsidy of one-half, as in Table 4-2, would probably be reasonably safe in this regard.

A third disadvantage of the WRS is difficulty of administration. To determine the transfer a person is entitled to, it is necessary to know both his wage rate and the number of hours he worked. For many people that information would be very hard to get—as a couple of examples will show. Waiters and waitresses are typical of people who are not employed at a fixed hourly wage rate, and it would be necessary to take account of tips, if that could be done, to arrive at their true hourly compensation. Self-employed people are likewise not employed at a fixed wage rate. What is the wage rate of a person who operates a small farm?

Another administrative problem involves the large incentives to cheat under the WRS. Consider a person who worked twenty hours at a wage rate of $3.00 per hour. If he could report his $60 income as resulting from forty hours of work at $1.50 an hour, he could receive a transfer of $30 (see Table 4-2). Even if the employer were held responsible for reporting hours and wage rates, there would be the possibility of employer-employee collusion to split the $30 gain from misreporting. It is not clear whether penalties could be applied and enforced to overcome the large gains that could be finagled by misreporting. And what could be done if two housewives agreed to do each others' housework at $.10 an hour?

Administrative problems were not covered in our discussion of the NIT, but of course that plan is not without its own difficulties in this regard. Cheating through underreporting of income could also occur under the NIT. However, the NIT's administrative problems may be less difficult to overcome than those of the WRS. Since the administrative problems of the NIT are similar to those of the federal income tax, the Internal Revenue Service has had plenty of experience with the kind of difficulties that would inevitably arise. Nonetheless, it has had little experience with low-income families, so the administration of an NIT could be more complex than that of current tax programs.

A final disadvantage of the WRS is that it would have to be accompanied by a companion policy to serve the nonworking poor. Some poor people are incapable of working, and a WRS would not benefit them at all. Provision has to be made for those who cannot work and for those who can only work part-time at wage rates not sufficient to support themselves. This means that the WRS would have to be coordinated with an income guarantee program. By contrast, the NIT could exist alone since it already has an income guarantee.

Ideally, a WRS could be applied to those who are able to work and a companion program, perhaps an NIT, could be restricted to those not able to work. If people could easily be placed in categories "able to work" and "unable to work," there would be no problem. Then the companion NIT program for the nonworking could use a sizeable guarantee and high marginal tax rates with no fear of producing disincentive effects. However, as we saw in the discussion of categorical cash transfers, there seems to be no straightforward and satisfactory way to make this type of distinction. But the fact that the distinction between those who are able and those who are unable to work cannot be made precisely does not mean that the WRS approach should be jettisoned: a rough categorization of people would still allow the work incentive features of the WRS to be realized for some families.

In fact, it might be possible to avoid having to classify groups as working versus nonworking by allowing families to classify themselves. If we had both an NIT and a WRS but allowed a family to receive benefits from only one program, then each family could choose for itself the program it would prefer. The disadvantage of this approach is that the income guarantee of the NIT would have to be kept fairly low to ensure that not too many families capable of working selected that program. In any case, the existence of the companion NIT would necessarily dilute the work incentive advantage of the WRS to some degree.

It is not easy to appraise all the difficulties of coordinating a WRS with a companion program without having a specific proposal in mind. But clearly there would be a number of problems that would necessitate unhappy compromises.

From this discussion, it is evident that the WRS has a number of defects in comparison with an NIT. The main advantage of a WRS is its work incentive feature, but that may be more than offset by its distributional effects, administrative difficulties, and problems of coordination with a companion policy. There is no way of assessing the magnitude of these disadvantages at the present time. While the WRS holds out the promise of avoiding a serious problem of the NIT, the effect on work incentives, it seems decidedly inferior in most other respects.

Substitute or Supplement?

By and large, our discussion of the NIT and the WRS has ignored the complications that would arise if either of these programs were to coexist with other transfer and tax policies. For analytical purposes, it was simply assumed that the well-being and economic incentives of recipients were affected only by the NIT or the WRS.

If the NIT were to become the 169th federal program, rather than replacing most of the present 168, an evaluation of its effects would be much more difficult. Given the immense variation in the eligibility rules of the present programs, some families might be receiving only NIT transfers, but most would be receiving these transfers plus benefits under food stamps, social security, SSI, medicare, medicaid, AFDC, or some combination of these programs and others. It would clearly not be possible to make general statements about the consequences of the NIT in this setting that would be accurate in all cases. However, present programs have one common characteristic, namely the high, but variable, marginal tax rates they impose on low-income families. As was pointed out in the last chapter, probably the lowest marginal tax rate imposed on poor families by these programs is in excess of 40 percent, and more commonly the rate exceeds 60 percent.

The addition of an NIT to the current system would unavoidably produce even higher combined marginal tax rates—exactly how much higher depending on whether other transfers were counted as income in determining the NIT transfer. For example, a family now receiving food stamps and paying both the social security tax and a 5 percent state income tax has an effective marginal tax rate of about 40 to 45 percent. If an NIT plan with a 50 percent marginal tax rate of its own were added, and if the family's food stamp transfer and tax payments were not deductible in computing the NIT transfer, the combined effect would be a marginal tax rate in excess of 90 percent. This would almost completely destroy work incentives. If deductions of other taxes and transfers were allowed, the combined marginal tax rate would be 72 percent—probably still high enough to have grave economic consequences. It would be very difficult to design any NIT plan that would provide sizeable transfers and avoid increasing the effective marginal tax rates to a very high level. And recall that we are discussing in this example a family that receives only food stamps. If the family receives transfers under other programs as well, tax rates would be even higher.

Milton Friedman has shown how adding an NIT to the present system can have calamitous results. In 1970, the House of Representatives passed a version of President Nixon's Family Assistance Plan (FAP), a form of NIT with an income guarantee for a family of four of $1,600. So as to ensure that families suffered no reduction in welfare payments as a result of FAP, the House bill required a state to supplement FAP payments if its existing support level for families of four was above $1,600. Table 4-3, which is based on Friedman's table, shows the results for a state that would be required to add $1,400 to the FAP payment to maintain its pre-FAP support level of $3,000.[17] (Eighteen states had programs paying at least that amount in 1970.) The combined effect of the transfers and taxes can be seen by comparing the top and bottom rows of Table 4-3. A family with a zero income before transfers would have had a dis-

Table 4-3
EFFECTS OF COMBINING FAP WITH SELECTED EXISTING TAX AND TRANSFER PROGRAMS, 1970, FAMILY OF FOUR

Income before transfers	$ 0	$ 720	$2,280	$3,600	$3,920	$5,003
Plus transfers from:						
Family Assistance Plan	1,600	1,600	820	160	0	0
State supplement	1,400	1,400	1,140	920	867	0
Food stamp program	372	156	0	0	0	0
Income after transfers	3,372	3,876	4,240	4,680	4,787	5,003
Minus taxes:						
Social security tax	0	35	109	173	188	240
Federal income tax	0	0	0	0	67	275
Disposable income	3,372	3,841	4,131	4,507	4,532	4,488

Source: Milton Friedman, "Welfare: Back to the Drawing Board," reprinted from *Newsweek* in *An Economist's Protest* (Glen Ridge, New Jersey: Thomas Horton and Co., 1972), p. 137.

posable income of $3,372. If it earned $720, its disposable income would have increased by $469, reflecting a marginal tax rate of 35 percent on the first $720 of earnings. The effective marginal tax rates were significantly higher at other income levels. On average, the marginal tax rate over the income range of $720 to $5,003 was 85 percent. By increasing its earnings from $720 to $5,003, or by $4,283, a family would have increased its disposable income by only $647. Even more noteworthy is the fact that the effective marginal tax rate was above 100 percent over a significant range of income. Note that a family earning $3,600 actually would have had a higher disposable income than a family earning $5,003.

Friedman did not even have to consider all existing transfer programs to show the folly of the approach taken in the House version of Nixon's FAP. For many families, there were other transfers and taxes which would have meant even higher marginal tax rates. Today, of course, with the expansion of the welfare system since 1970, it would be even more difficult to avoid unacceptably high marginal tax rates. And recall that work incentives are not the only problem associated with high marginal tax rates: the problems of "tax loopholes" and human capital investment also are intensified by high rates.

Friedman is certainly correct in stressing that an NIT should be used as a substitute for existing programs: "A negative income tax— which is what the Family Assistance Plan is—makes sense only if it replaces at least some of our present rag bag of programs. It makes no sense if it is simply piled on other programs." [18]

As with the NIT, a WRS plan could not easily be added to the present system of welfare programs. With respect to the incentive to work, however, it coordinates with the present system better than does the NIT. Basically, this is because the WRS embodies negative marginal tax rates on work effort, and those negative rates would tend to offset the positive marginal tax rates of other programs. Consider a worker subject to an initial 45 percent marginal tax rate. For such a worker with a market wage rate of $2.00, the WRS of Table 4-2 would provide a supplement of $.50 an hour. An extra hour of work would increase the WRS transfer by $.50, but the 45 percent marginal tax rate in other programs would reduce net transfers under those programs by $.90 for that extra hour worked at the $2.00 rate. The combined effect would produce a net wage rate of $1.60 ($2.00 + $.50 − $.90), or an effective marginal tax rate on the market wage rate of only 20 percent. So adding the WRS actually reduced the effective marginal tax rate of other programs, which was 45 percent in this case, to 20 percent. The exact amount of the reduction depends on the worker's market wage rate and on what other transfers and tax policies are involved.

Unfortunately, the offsetting feature of the WRS applies only to extra earnings generated by more work. Extra earnings generated by higher market wage rates would be "taxed" very heavily, since workers would lose benefits from the WRS as well as from other programs. In the example, if the worker moved from a job paying $2.00 an hour to one paying $2.50, his net wage rate would increase from $1.60 to only $1.63. In other words, workers would have almost no incentive to seek out the highest paying jobs available and this would seriously undermine the ability of labor markets to efficiently allocate the labor services of affected workers. (It also leaves little incentive to improve job skills.) When the administrative and distributional effects of the WRS are also considered, it becomes clear that the consequences of adding the WRS to the present welfare system would be unlikely, on balance, to be favorable.

Either a WRS (with a companion policy for those unable to work) or an NIT can replace most existing programs. As replacements, there is much to be said for these programs, but as additions they would probably have disastrous effects. In fact, it is unlikely that there are any small changes in the present system that would represent substantial improvements. The present system is so complicated and has so many inequities and misdirected incentives that piecemeal reform would be a hazardous undertaking. Instead, in my opinion, reform should begin with the recognition that the present system must be largely discarded if meaningful progress is to be made. Whether a WRS (with a companion policy) or an NIT would be the preferable replacement is not clear. I tend to favor the NIT, but further research may show that the shortcomings of the WRS approach are less serious than they now appear.

CHAPTER V

THE VOLUME OF REDISTRIBUTION

It is not possible to prove scientifically what constitutes the most desirable amount of redistribution. The very term desirable implies a subjective affirmation that a certain course of action is the preferred one, and that affirmation, in turn, requires a nonscientific value judgment. If $1,000 is taken from individual A and given to individual B, there is no way to determine whether the net effect is to produce a "better" society. However, this does not mean that economics can contribute nothing to resolving the question of how much redistribution is desirable. It can help by pointing out some of the objective consequences of redistribution which, when coupled with a person's values, can form the basis for a more informed opinion. The modest aim of this chapter is to stress some of the effects of redistribution that I believe most people would want to consider when formulating opinions on this matter.

Any redistribution tends to improve the standard of living of recipients at the expense of taxpayers. This, however, does not necessarily mean that the taxpayers are worse off. Recently, a number of economists have emphasized that transferring income to low-income families may actually benefit those who give up the resources that finance the redistribution. Higher incomes for the poor may benefit other people in a number of ways. Making the poor better off, for example, might help reduce crime, juvenile delinquency, or social unrest. There are also the less tangible benefits that result from feelings of altruism on the part of those more fortunately situated in the income distribution. No doubt many people are willing to pay, say, $1,000 in taxes as their share of a $20 billion redistribution to the poor. Those who are well-off may care about the living standards of others and be willing to pay taxes to help improve the lot of low-income families.[1]

These indirect benefits felt by higher-income families are instances of the external benefits of redistribution. To my mind, these and similar reasons provide a strong argument for having the government engage in redistribution. Unfortunately, they do not provide much guidance in deciding exactly how much redistribution is warranted, in part because we have very little knowledge about the quantitative importance of these external benefits. One authority on redistribution, Lester Thurow, has observed: "If social unrest, crime, riots, and other such phenomena are caused by maldistributions of economic resources, then these undesirable social events can be eliminated by altering the distribution of economic resources." However, Thurow then went on to note: "There is little or no empirical evidence (economic, sociological, or psychological) showing such a connection."[2] If this conclusion concerning the more tangible external benefits of redistribution is correct, we are left to evaluate the less tangible benefits, that is, the good feelings that the well-off receive from knowing they are helping the poor. But no one knows whether these benefits are substantial, or even if they exist.

Out of necessity, then, this chapter will not devote much space to speculation about the indirect benefits of redistribution. Instead, it will emphasize some less esoteric, but more practical, considerations.

On the Cost of Redistribution

When people speak of the cost of a redistributive plan, they most frequently mean the net amount of redistribution the plan would accomplish. Thus, when the cost of a particular NIT plan is said to be $10 billion, this usually means that $10 billion is the sum of the transfers that would be made to families below the breakeven income. Such estimates are often quite ambiguous. If the breakeven income is above the level of zero taxable income in the federal income tax, this figure would understate the actual amount of redistribution. As we saw, coordination of the NIT with the federal income tax necessitates reduced taxes for some families, and these reductions, like the transfers themselves, must be financed by families above the tax breakeven level of income. But in the case of many NIT proposals, it is not clear whether the published cost estimates include reduced taxes or not. Another ambiguity is that some cost estimates assume that the NIT would replace other (often unspecified) transfer programs, and the savings resulting from the elimination of these programs are subtracted to arrive at the net cost. Moreover, almost all cost estimates assume that there would be no reductions in earnings in response to the plan.

For these reasons, cost estimates of the usual type must be interpreted with care. Even so, it is very difficult for a person to know whether a given cost should be considered heavy, moderate, or light. A $4,000–50 percent NIT (family of four) was estimated to have a net cost of $27.5 billion in 1971,[3] and a $5,500–50 percent NIT was widely cited as costing $71 billion at about the same time.[4] In inflationary times, when people are accustomed to thinking in terms of ever larger numbers, it is difficult to know whether such programs should be viewed as imposing heavy or moderate burdens. Sometimes such cost estimates are related to gross national product: the cheaper of the above NIT plans would have redistributed 2.5 percent of GNP in 1971, and even the more expensive one would have redistributed only 6.5 percent. Viewed in relation to the total output of the economy, these programs do not appear to be prohibitively large.

Yet I intend to show that, when viewed properly, programs of this size are much more difficult to finance than is commonly realized. Indeed, it is my contention that the more expensive of the above NIT plans would have strained the very ability of the American economic system to function, since it would have imposed marginal tax rates in excess of 80 percent on all families in the United States. That a program costing only 6.5 percent of GNP could have such an effect may seem incredible—which is all the more reason for understanding why it is true.

In order to understand the difficulty of financing a redistributive program, it is essential to see how it will affect both the marginal and the average tax rates of all families, but especially the marginal tax rates. While this cannot be done with precision, it is possible to obtain a rough idea of what is involved by assuming that the redistribution occurs through the use of demogrants.[5] To simplify the analysis, we can begin by making three assumptions, the first two of which we will drop later: (1) the only government expenditure program is the demogrant program, (2) all families are of the same size, and (3) the demogrants are financed by a proportional (flat-rate) tax on pretransfer income—with no deductions, exemptions, or exclusions allowed. To finance demogrants of any significant size it is essential to have a large tax base. Since we are interested in what is *possible*, we shall use the largest tax base available—the total income of the economy. If high tax rates on this base are required, then even higher rates would be necessary on real-world tax bases, for they are not as comprehensive.

Figure 5-1

EFFECT OF HYPOTHETICAL DEMOGRANT ON TAX STRUCTURE

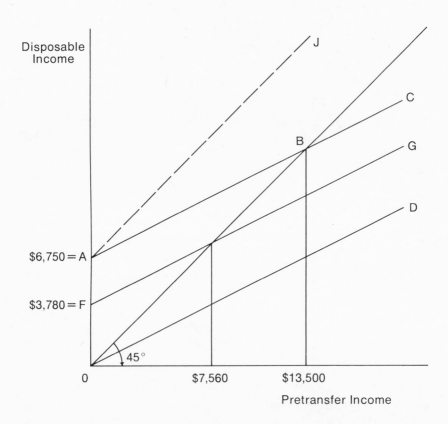

These assumptions make it easy to calculate the tax rate required to finance any demogrant. Suppose we wish to pay to each family a demogrant equal to one-half of average family income. Total outlays on demogrants would then be one-half the average family income times the total number of families, or exactly one-half of total income in the community. To finance such an outlay on demogrants would necessitate raising tax revenue equal to one-half of total family income, implying a required tax rate of 50 percent. The outcome is illustrated in Figure 5-1. Assume that average (not median) family income is $13,500—which is approximately the figure given by the Cenus Bureau for 1973. A demogrant to each family of half of $13,500, or $6,750, is shown by the dotted line AJ. The 50 percent tax is shown by OD, and the net relationship between disposable income and pretransfer income is shown by line ABC. Note that this scheme does not affect the disposable income of a family with an average income; that family pays taxes equal to half its income and receives a demogrant also equal to half its income. Thus, the net schedule ABC passes through the point on the 45 degree line indicating average family income. Under our assumptions, this is always true for any demogrant financed by a proportional tax on total family income.

The net effect of the demogrants and taxes is to redistribute income from those with above average incomes to those with below average incomes. Exactly how much income is redistributed cannot be determined without knowing the distribution of families along the income scale. For example, if all families had an income equal to the average, this demogrant plan would not redistribute any income at all, for every family would then pay a tax equal to half its income and receive a transfer of exactly the same size in return. On the other hand, if half the families had pretransfer incomes of $27,000 and half had incomes of zero, this plan would redistribute one-fourth of the total income of the economy. In general, the more unequal the distribution of income, the larger the net redistribution accomplished by a given plan. But the required marginal tax rate does not depend on the actual distribution of income: for a demogrant equal to half the average income, that rate is 50 percent regardless of how unequal, or equal, the distribution happens to be.

In the example above it was assumed that the demogrant was equal to one-half of the average income. (Alternatively, we could have examined how to finance a $6,750–50 percent NIT plan with a flat rate tax on income above the breakeven income, since this plan would have identical results.) We saw that this required a marginal tax rate of 50 percent. If, instead, we had set the demogrant at two-thirds of average income, the same reasoning shows that the required tax rate would be 66⅔ percent. This approach has the advantage of making it very simple to determine the tax rate that is required: in all cases, under our assumptions, the tax rate equals the ratio of the demogrant (or income guarantee) to average family income.

Now it can be seen why it may be misleading to give the net cost (that is, how much is redistributed) of a redistributive plan as a percent of NNP (total income). Based on the actual distribution of families along the income scale in the United States, I estimate that the net redistribution of the 50-percent demogrant would be roughly 10 percent of total income. In other words, for every 1 percent of total income redistributed in this way, the marginal tax rate for all families must be raised by about five percentage points.[6] There are two reasons for this: First, all income in the economy is not available for financing the *net* redistribution, since only income above the average can be taxed to provide the funds to be redistributed downward. Second, greater redistribution means higher tax rates must be applied to the recipients as well as to those who finance the redistribution.

Stating the cost of a redistributive program as a percent of total income, then, can give a very misleading impression about the difficulty of financing the transfers. Another way to make the cost of such programs appear moderate is to emphasize average tax rates instead of marginal tax rates. For the plan discussed above, the average tax rate (total taxes less transfers as a percent of income) for a family with an average income is zero, since its disposable income is unaffected. Even at an income of $27,000, the average tax rate is only 25 percent. But the marginal tax rate for both of these families, and all others, would be 50 percent.

It must be stressed that it is the marginal tax rate that is crucial in evaluating the economic impact of such plans. This was emphasized for the NIT in the last chapter, and it is no less true for a positive income tax.[7] How much a person gets to keep out of each extra dollar of earnings is an important factor affecting individual decisions on work effort. High marginal tax rates can cause taxpayers as well as transfer recipients to reduce work effort. And it is not only work incentives that will be affected, but also the incentive to save and invest (including investment in human capital) and the incentive to convert income into nontaxable forms (that is, to use tax loopholes). All of these effects depend largely on the marginal tax rate.

The important question is: how high can marginal tax rates go before these distortions outweigh the advantages of further redistribution? If we increase the marginal tax rate from 50 to 60 percent, we can set an income guarantee of 60 percent of average income. But suppose the higher tax rate leads to a 20-percent reduction in average income, lowering it from $13,500 to $10,800. Then the income guarantee would be $6,480—actually less than it is with the 50-percent tax rate. (Thinking of the disincentive effects in terms of a reduction in average income is simply a shorthand way of expressing the longer-run damage to economic growth—because of less saving and less investment in human capital—and the greater use of tax loopholes.) Unfortunately, it is not known just how responsive people are to higher marginal tax rates. But it is clear that, at some point, attempting to redistribute more can become counterproductive because of the consequences of the high marginal tax rates that must be used.

One thing is known about the economic damage done by the distorting effect of tax rates: the damage increases in proportion to the square of the marginal tax rate. Basically, this is because low tax rates distort only marginal economic decisions, that is, those involving benefits only slightly in excess of costs, whereas high tax rates interfere with more important decisions.[8] To put this in perspective, it means that the additional damage done by raising the marginal tax rate from 50 percent to 51 percent, or by only one percentage point, is more than the total damage done by raising the tax rate from zero to 10 percent. And the additional damage caused by raising the marginal tax rate from 50 percent to 60 percent is greater than all the damage caused when the tax rate is initially increased from zero to 33 percent. In addition, the 60-percent tax rate would redistribute only about 2 percent more of total income—assuming *no* reduction in average income—and only half of this would go to families with incomes below one-half the median family income.

In view of these considerations, it appears to me that marginal tax rates of 50 percent are about as high as we should go. I am sure this opinion would not be shared by all economists: some would say the figure should be lower, and others would put it higher. The source of these differences in opinion is largely based on differing judgments as to the impact of high marginal tax rates on economic productivity. For those who believe that work, saving, and investment are not affected significantly by pecuniary incentives, the limit to which we could raise marginal tax rates would appear higher. (Saying that the damage done by taxes varies with the square of the marginal tax rate does not imply exactly how large the damage is for any given rate.) For purposes of focusing the following discussion, it will be assumed that 50 percent is a reasonable maximum for the marginal tax rate, but the reader can easily make adjustments if he feels the figure should be higher or lower.

The assumption that the marginal tax rate must not exceed 50 percent limits the income guarantee per family to half of average family income. But so far our discussion has assumed that government spends only to redistribute income. In fact, much of government spending is on programs of general benefit, such as defense, highways, police, environmental matters, and interest on the public debt. Indeed, in 1973, non-social welfare expenditures plus education amounted to 22 percent of net national product. (For reasons discussed in Chapter 2, I will consider education as a non-redistributional program.) Such a high level of expenditure significantly limits how much redistribution can be accomplished, since 22 percent of total income (assuming that income for tax purposes is defined broadly enough to equal NNP, although that is not fully feasible) must be taxed away to finance these general programs. With a limit of 50 percent on the effective marginal tax rate, this means that only 28 percent of total money income is available to finance demogrants. Thus, the income guarantee can only be 28 percent of average income, or only $3,780. The effective schedule relating disposable income and pretransfer income then becomes FG in Figure 5-1, with an income guarantee of $3,780 and a breakeven income of $7,560.

Taking account of government non-redistributive expenditures thus has a crucial effect on the size of the transfers that can be made to low-income families. The larger the spending on general programs, the smaller the amount of redistribution possible as long as we accept a limit on the effective marginal tax rate. That an income guarantee of just over a fourth of average income is as high as we can go may seem surprising. Recall that originally the poverty lines were set at about one-half of median family income. But one-half of the median income is about 45 percent of average income, so to finance a guarantee at that level plus other expenditures equal to 22 percent of NNP would require, under our assumptions, marginal tax rates of at least 67 percent. (I say at least, because this conclusion assumes, probably incorrectly, that it is feasible to tax a base as large as NNP. In all likelihood, marginal tax rates would have to exceed 70 percent.)

It might be thought that the reason for this surprising conclusion is our assumption of a proportional tax. It is true that if a progressive tax were used, the same income guarantee could be financed with lower tax rates for low- and middle-income families, and higher marginal rates for high-income families. But this does not significantly alter our conclusion. Suppose we enacted the $3,780–50 percent program illustrated in Figure 5-1 and decided to finance it by levying higher taxes on the wealthy in order to lower the rate below 50 percent for other people. In 1970, the total adjusted gross income (AGI: the broadest measure of income available from income tax statistics) [9] for taxpayers with AGI above $100,000 was $14.4 billion. An increase in their tax rates from one-half to two-thirds would raise only $2 billion in extra revenue, which would permit us to reduce the marginal rate for those below $100,000 from 50 percent to about 49.7 percent. If we applied the two-thirds rate to taxpayers with adjusted gross incomes above $50,000 (whose total AGI was $37.5 billion), [10] this would raise an extra $7 billion and would permit the marginal tax rate on those below $50,000 to be reduced only to about 49 percent.

What these facts make clear is that taxing the wealthy very heavily will not permit a significant lightening of the tax burden for the remainder of the population. There are simply too few wealthy taxpayers to make much difference: less than 1 percent of all taxpayers have adjusted gross incomes above $50,000. So any major redistribution of income cannot avoid heavy taxation of families in the middle- and upper-middle income range.

Now let us relate this analysis to the situation that actually existed in the United States in 1973. In Chapter 2, I presented estimates that implied transfers to the lowest income households of about $1,500 per capita (see page 24). This redistribution would average $6,000 per family of four, but $6,000 was 44 percent of average family income in 1973. If our earlier analysis in this chapter is correct, financing an income guarantee of 44 percent of average income plus general expenditures equal to about 22 percent of total income would require a marginal tax rate of 66 percent. But it is clear that very few families face marginal tax rates approaching that figure. There appears to be a major contradiction between the estimates in Chapter 2 and the analysis here.

Actually, these figures can be reconciled. A large part of the explanation lies in the fact that our assumption that all families are of the same size is not correct. In fact, low-income families tend to be smaller than average. Among those officially classified as poor in 1972, average family size (counting unrelated individuals as families of one) was about three persons. In contrast, the average family size of those in the upper 80 percent of the income distribution was slightly larger—about three-and-a-half persons. Therefore, the income guarantee for the average poor family, composed of three persons, would be $4,500 instead of $6,000. It is interesting to note that the fortuitous fact that average family size is smaller for low-income families than for the whole society has enabled us to redistribute more on a per capita basis than would otherwise be the case.

Since $4,500 is 33 percent of average family income, the required marginal tax rate is only 55 percent. But this still overstates the difficulty of financing the redistribution that occurred in 1973. The $13,500 average money income figure is well below the average real income of American families. There are a number of reasons for this. One is that money income is underreported in the Census Bureau survey. In addition, realized capital gains and retained corporate earnings are not counted. More important, the Census Bureau reports income after some taxes have been paid, and for computations of the type we are making before-tax income must be used. The major culprits here are employer contributions to social security and corporate income taxes; in effect, these taxes take part of income before it reaches the paycheck or dividend check. Adjusting the $13,500 figure for these excluded items of real income yields an average before-tax income of about $18,000. American families are a lot wealthier, at least before taxes, than is suggested by the frequently cited Census Bureau figures.

The $4,500 effective income guarantee in 1973 was 25 percent of before-tax average income of $18,000. Adding 22 percent to finance non-social welfare programs gives an effective marginal tax rate of 47 percent. Thus, the effective income guarantee in 1973 would have required a marginal tax rate of almost 50 percent on all families if it had been provided in the form of demogrants. It is no easier to finance the guarantee, of course, if it is provided by means of a multitude of different welfare programs instead of demogrants—although it is possible for some families to face marginal rates lower than 47 percent, but only if rates are higher for other families. So, if we accept the 50 percent limit to the effective marginal tax rate, it appears that the United States was approaching the limit of its ability to redistribute income in 1973.

This conclusion may appear surprising, especially in light of the fact that most families are not aware of marginal tax rates anywhere close to 50 percent. The feeling that tax rates are not that high is partly illusory, though, and is due to the fact that many taxes are hidden. It is also partly correct, since probably only low-income families faced marginal tax rates of that magnitude. In fact, the main reason why most middle-income families probably had a marginal tax rate lower than 50 percent was that low-income families had rates well above 50 percent. Figure 5-2 attempts to give a rough picture of what the actual tax-transfer process in the United States looked like in 1973. The net relationship between disposable income and pretransfer income (that is, income before taxes and transfers defined so that average income is $18,000) is shown by ABCD. Net transfers were paid between pretransfer income of zero and $6,900, and the marginal tax rate (MTR) was about 65 percent up to $8,000 or so. It is this very high marginal tax rate which permits lower rates at higher income levels. Even so, between incomes of $8,000 and $18,000, the rate was probably at least 35 percent, rising to 40 percent and above for higher incomes. The dotted line shows what the relationship would have been if a 47 percent proportional tax had been used to finance a demogrant of $4,500 per family plus other non-social welfare expenditures.

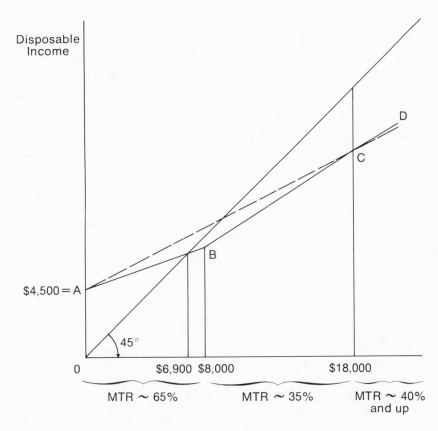

Figure 5-2

THE U.S. TAX-TRANSFER SYSTEM, 1973

Disposable
Income

$4,500 = A

45°

0    $6,900 $8,000 $18,000

MTR ∼ 65%   MTR ∼ 35%   MTR ∼ 40%
and up

It must be emphasized that this is an imprecise picture of a very complex situation. As a broad overview, I think it is substantially correct, but it depicts broad averages and not individual cases. Thus, many families with incomes below $6,900 may not have received any transfers at all, and these families would have had marginal tax rates well below 65 percent. But many other families received transfers under several programs and paid several taxes. For families like these, effective marginal tax rates could have been well above 65 percent. When it is recognized that a family receiving only food stamps faces a marginal tax rate of about 40 to 45 percent and that food stamps are only one small program in the social welfare category, this 65 percent figure should appear more plausible.

It may also be surprising to see tax rates of 35 percent and above for families with pretransfer incomes in the middle income ranges.

However, since total taxes as a percent of NNP were about 35 percent in 1973, these figures are not likely to be too high. If they look high it is because most people think of their marginal tax bracket in terms of the federal income tax only. But the relevant marginal tax rate is the combined effect of that tax plus all others. Consider a family in a 20 percent federal tax bracket. Such a family probably also pays a social security tax of almost 12 percent and state and local income and/or sales taxes that probably add 5 percent more. This brings the effective marginal tax rate above 35 percent. If any of the income left after paying these taxes is used to invest in capital (subject to the corporate income tax), to purchase housing (subject to the property tax), or to purchase any of the goods on which excise taxes are levied, then it is clear that the *effective* marginal tax rate easily can exceed 40 percent. To repeat, the fact that taxes take 35 percent of NNP guarantees that most families will face effective rates in excess of that figure.

Thus, the only way the United States avoids marginal tax rates of nearly 50 percent for all families is by subjecting those with low incomes to even higher rates. This is not entirely illogical from an economic standpoint. Since the entire pretax income of the lowest quartile is not more than $30 or $35 billion, even if disincentive effects cut this figure in half, the loss in total output would only be 1 or 2 percent of NNP. But the total pretax income of the upper three quartiles is in excess of $1,000 billion. Even a 2 or 3 percent reduction here because of tax-induced distortions would cause a greater reduction in total output than a 50 percent reduction for the lowest quartile. Therefore, this type of graduated rate structure—with the highest marginal rates on low-income families—makes sense. Subjecting low-income families to high marginal tax rates is simply the price paid for maintaining incentives at higher-income levels and thus ensuring a large total output. A large total output, in turn, is essential if we are to continue financing the large net transfers to low-income families.

If we admit the possibility of using marginal tax rates above 50 percent for low-income families, our conclusion that the United States cannot redistribute any greater volume of resources than it now does no longer holds. But it would still be very difficult to redistribute significantly more to low-income families, unless we subject them to tax rates even above 65 percent. To redistribute an additional 2 percent of NNP would require that marginal tax rates for all income levels rise by 10 percentage points. And if we do not allow the rate to rise above 65 percent for low-income families, then it must rise by even more than 10 percentage points for higher-income families. In that event, most of the net redistribution would go to families not in the lowest 20 or 25 percent of the income distribution, and almost all families with incomes in excess of $8,000 would be subjected to tax rates of at least 50 percent. It is far from clear that redistribution of this sort would be worth its cost.

Our proposition concerning the difficulty of redistributing additional resources to the low-income population must be understood in a relative sense. In time, as all incomes rise, it will be possible for the same marginal tax rate structure to finance larger transfers without raising the rates, but what will not be possible without higher rates is to have an effective income guarantee that is a larger proportion of average income. In 1973, a $4,500 effective guarantee for a family of three was about one-third of average income as reported by the Census Bureau. To go much beyond one-third would require marginal tax rates exceeding 50 percent for a large segment, if not all, of the population. Stated differently, in 1973 the net transfer to the lowest quartile was about 6 percent of NNP; to raise that by an additional percentage point would almost certainly require that marginal tax rates rise by more than 10 percentage points for the upper three quartiles, since more than 1 percent of NNP must be redistributed to get that additional amount into the hands of families in the lowest quartile.

While these general conclusions are based on very rough estimates, Benjamin Okner's recent empirical study of demogrants supports these results.[11] Using data from 1970, Okner examined the distributional effects of several alternative demogrant plans. Two of his plans, Plan B and Plan D, are described in Table 5-1. These plans are of roughly the same magnitude, with total outlays estimated at $215.4 billion for Plan B and $200.7 billion for Plan D. (Recall that gross outlays do not measure the net redistribution of a demogrant program.) Even though Plan B involves a smaller grant to a family of four, it costs more than Plan D because it makes larger grants to smaller-sized families.

Okner assumed that the federal income tax would be used to finance these plans. He also assumed that virtually all "loopholes" had been eliminated thereby providing for an expanded tax base, and increasing taxable income by more than 70 percent. This broadened tax base not only is in accord with our earlier assumption that all family income would be subject to tax, but also is essential—for it would be almost impossible to finance these plans out of taxable income as it is now defined. In addition, Okner assumed that demogrants had replaced several federal transfer programs involving expenditures of $7.5 billion in 1970. Since I

Table 5-1
OUTLAYS, TAX RATES AND NET REDISTRIBUTION UNDER TWO ALTERNATIVE DEMOGRANT PLANS, 1970

	Plan B	Plan D
Amount of demogrant		
Single person	$1,500	$1,250
Married couple, no children	3,000	2,500
Married couple, two children	3,600	4,000
Total outlays on demogrants (billions)	$215.4	$200.7
Federal income tax rate (after comprehensive reform)	42.2%	40.2%
Net redistribution (billions)	$ 47.0	$ 45.3

Source: U.S. Congress, Joint Economic Committee, Subcommittee on Fiscal Policy, *Studies in Public Welfare,* Paper No. 9, 93rd Congress, 1st session, November 1973. A study on "The Role of Demogrants as an Income Maintenance Alternative," by Benjamin A. Okner, Table 1.

estimate (using the procedure described in Chapter 2) that the net transfer to the lowest quartile of the income distribution in 1970 was about $50 billion, this means that Okner allowed the demogrants to replace only 15 percent of the redistribution that took place in 1970. For all practical purposes, then, he was simply estimating the effect of adding these demogrant plans on top of all the other tax and transfer programs existing in 1970.

The federal income tax yielded $83.8 billion in tax revenue in 1970. To finance Okner's demogrant plans, it would have had to have raised this sum, plus the outlays on demogrants and minus the $7.5 billion in eliminated expenditures—that is, a total of $291.7 billion assuming Plan B and $277 billion assuming Plan D. Using the broadened tax base, tax rates of 42.2 and 40.2 percent would have been required.

But these tax rates are only those for the federal income tax. Actually, in 1970 the federal income tax raised only one-fourth of all tax revenue; other federal, state, and local taxes accounted for 25 percent of net national product. If we assume that in some way a tax base as broad as NNP could be used, then the marginal tax rate due to these other taxes would have been 25 percent. Adding this to the federal income tax rates gives effective marginal tax rates of 65 percent for Plan D and 67 percent for Plan B. And this ignores the fact that some of the other transfer programs had implicit tax rates of their own. For many low-income families this would have meant that effective marginal tax rates would have exceeded 80 percent. Also, these calculations assume no reductions in work effort as a result of the demogrants. If disincentive effects were important and total income fell, even higher tax rates would be required to finance the same outlays.

The net redistribution accomplished by any demogrant plan is far below the gross outlays made. Okner estimated the net redistribution of Plan B at $47.0 billion and that of Plan D at $45.3 billion. Roughly speaking, these would have been the amounts transferred from families with above average incomes to those below. Converting these figures to percentages of NNP, Plan B would have redistributed 5.3 percent of NNP and Plan D, 5.1 percent. Note that this tends to verify our earlier conclusions that marginal tax rates must rise by five percentage points for each percent of NNP redistributed. Since effective marginal tax rates in the absence of these programs were probably around 40 percent for most families except the low-income population, the redistribution of about 5 percent of NNP would have increased these rates by twenty-five to twenty-seven percentage points.

Not all of this net redistribution would have gone to low-income families. In fact, only $14.7 billion of the $47 billion redistributed by Plan B and only $12 billion of the $45.3 billion redistributed by Plan D would have reached the lowest quartile of the income distribution.[12] Since the net transfer to the lowest quartile in 1970 was $50 billion to begin with, these demogrants would have increased the net transfer by only one-fourth. It should be recalled that it is a virtual necessity for most of any additional redistribution to accrue to the broad middle-income range when we start with large transfers already being made to the lowest quartile. The only way to avoid this is to use much higher marginal tax rates on low-income families.

Okner concluded that these demogrant plans were "economically feasible." It is not clear what he meant by this, but his calculations did assume that there would be no disincentive effects at all from the grants. In addition, he completely ignored all taxes except the federal income tax, even though the burden of other taxes was three times as great as the income tax in 1970. In my opinion, programs which would impose effective marginal tax rates of close to 70 percent are not feasible: I would expect serious disincentive effects to result from tax rates that high.

Table 5-2 reports the distributional effects of these programs (again assuming no disincentive effects, of course) in a different form. The first column gives the estimated percentage distribution

Table 5-2

EFFECTS OF TWO DEMOGRANT PLANS ON PERCENTAGE DISTRIBUTION OF MONEY INCOME, 1970

	Income after Taxes and Transfers, 1970	Income after Taxes and Transfers	
		Plan B	Plan D
Lowest quintile	5.29%	7.01%	6.70%
Second quintile	8.84	10.76	10.54
Third quintile	14.97	16.41	16.45
Fourth quintile	23.27	23.08	23.24
Highest quintile	47.63	42.74	43.07

Source: U.S. Congress, Joint Economic Committee, Subcommittee on Fiscal Policy, *Studies in Public Welfare*, Paper No. 9, 93rd Congress, 1st session, November 1973. A study on "The Role of Demogrants as an Income Maintenance Alternative," by Benjamin A. Okner, Table 6.

by quintiles for 1970. (These figures do not agree with those of Table 2-2 because Okner did not use Census Bureau data; he also used a different definition of income, and he included unrelated individuals as well as families in the breakdown by families.) The striking aspect of these figures is the apparently modest changes wrought by the demogrants. Plan B increases the percentage share of the lowest quintile by only 1.7 points, and Plan D by only 1.4 points. This view of the programs, which suggests that only modest changes are involved in the income distribution and the tax system, is highly misleading. In effect, Table 5-2 focuses on average tax rates instead of the more important (for purposes of economic incentives) marginal tax rates. Thus, our analysis suggests that it will be very difficult to bring about even small changes in the percentage distribution of income through such tax and transfer policies.

Okner's estimates also make it easy to get a rough idea of how costly the plan proposed by the National Welfare Rights Organization in 1969 would have been. The NWRO proposed, as an alternative to the Family Assistance Plan, an income guarantee of $5,500 for a family of four. By simply increasing the cost of Okner's Plan B by 50 percent, which would produce an income guarantee of $5,400, we can estimate approximately how difficult it would have been to finance the NWRO plan. It would have required gross outlays for demogrants of $322 billion and, on Okner's broadened tax base, an income tax rate (in 1970) of 58 percent. Taking account of the rates of other taxes, the effective marginal tax rate would have been about 83 percent, assuming no disincentive effects. This plan was widely cited as involving a net cost (presumably, net redistribution) of $71 billion. Although this was only 8 percent of NNP, the program would probably have produced economic ruin. Yet very few people seemed to comprehend this. Certainly Senator Eugene McCarthy did not, since he introduced legislation incorporating the NWRO proposal.

Several conclusions can be drawn from the analysis in this section:

First, in discussing redistributive programs it is essential to view the tax-transfer process in its entirety. The effective marginal tax rates that result from the combined effects of all taxes and transfers are the crucial indicators of the economic effects of these programs. This point has, of course, been emphasized at several places in the present study.

Second, to redistribute even 1 percent of NNP in addition to what is already being redistributed will typically require an increase in the marginal tax rates of all families of about five percentage points. (Of course, it would be possible to have marginal tax rates for *some* families rise by less than five percentage points if the program is structured so that marginal tax rates for other families rise by more than five percentage points.) Of this redistribution, only a portion can feasibly be concentrated on low-income families. Thus, the economic cost of distortions due to higher marginal tax rates at all levels of income would be quite large in comparison to the transfers actually made to low-income families. Whether this cost should be judged as too high to pay must be regarded as an open question.

Third, it is important that people understand the difficulties involved in financing major redistributions of income. To treat a proposal like that of the NWRO as responsible and realistic can only serve to inflate the expectations of low-income families far beyond the point where the economic system can fulfill them. This can only lead to bitterness and frustration on the part of both low-income families and well-intentioned reformers. There are some unpalatable but nonetheless inescapable truths in the economics of redistribution, and if we are to choose feasible policies they should be fully understood.

Money Income and Equality

To many observers, it seems obvious that taking money from those who have a good deal and giving it to those who have less produces a more just distribution of income. The belief that a more equal distribution is necessarily more equitable provides the motivation for much of the intellectual support for redistributive policies. Yet, focusing on inequalities in money incomes to the exclusion of all else reflects a very narrow view of equity. In fact, inequalities in money income are not only compatible with, but are absolutely essential for, the attainment of equity in a meaningful sense.

Let us suppose that all people have identical abilities to earn incomes and possess equal amounts of capital. Nonetheless, if their tastes and attitudes differ, the operation of a market system will produce substantial inequalities in annual money incomes. Insofar as these inequalities result from the free choices of people as they select the lifestyles most satisfactorily reflecting their preferences, I suspect that these inequalities would not be regarded as unjust. A significant part of the inequality we observe is of this type.

Consider the ways in which different preferences about money income and leisure affect annual money incomes. Ultimately, people choose how much of an effort to make to acquire income. The person who chooses to become a teacher and to work eight months a year for $8,000 has expressed a strong preference for leisure. If we could put a value on leisure time, that person's income might be equivalent to the income of someone else who makes $12,000 by working all year long. Of course, when we call time not spent at work "leisure," we are using a shorthand term for all non-money income-generating uses of time. Understood in this way, leisure is clearly an important part of a person's real income.

Most people, since they mistakenly think of everyone as working a forty-hour week (that is, possessing equal leisure time), tend to underestimate the importance of different tastes for leisure as a source of inequality in money incomes. Actually, two of the major sources of differential incomes are frequently overlooked: working wives and retirement. If we compare two couples, one with both husband and wife working and the other with only the husband working, we are likely to find a significant difference in money income. But this does not mean that their real incomes differ: the non-employed wife is simply indicating a preference for leisure (more accurately, perhaps, a preference for self-employment at home with payment in kind) over money income. Similarly, the retirement decision is generally a voluntary choice to substitute leisure for money income. Retired persons tend to have low money incomes on average, but they have much more leisure time than those who work.

It is also not fully appropriate to compare the money incomes of people who spend the same amount of time working. A more demanding or dangerous job, for example, must pay more to attract workers than a routine, secure job. Unequal money wage rates are often necessary to compensate for differences in the attractiveness of jobs. A person who could become a long-haul truck driver at $15,000 a year but decides to become a clerk at $9,000 is not necessarily irrational: he is simply showing that he considers the extra $6,000 insufficient compensation for what he feels to be the relative hardships of truck driving. Of course, a person who makes the opposite choice is not necessarily irrational either: he simply has different tastes. But in this case justice certainly does not require redistributing income from truck drivers to clerks.

A different problem arises from the use of one year as the appropriate time period for estimating a person's relative economic position. Two people may have very unequal incomes in any given year, but equal lifetime incomes. For example, a professional athlete may have a much higher income than a medical student one year, and the reverse could be true twenty years later, but both could have the same lifetime incomes. Similarly, to compare a young person just beginning his career to one who is in his prime earning years may give a spurious appearance of inequality. Age and experience are important sources of measured inequality since people typically have low incomes both early and late in life and high incomes during middle age. For instance, in 1972 the median income was $7,447 for families headed by a person in the age class of fourteen to twenty-four and $14,056 for families headed by a person in the age class of forty-five to fifty-four. For families headed by those over sixty-five years old, the median income was $5,968. Comparing people of different ages can thus give a false appearance of inequality. Redistribution from high- to low-income families would, in part, transfer income from middle-aged people to both the young and the old. Yet the typical young person is almost certain to have a higher lifetime income than the average middle-aged person, even in the absence of redistribution. This is because the economy grows over time, and per capita incomes rise correspondingly. By the time today's twenty-year-old reaches age fifty, the median income of the forty-five to fifty-four-year-old class will probably be at least $20,000, so the lifetime income of the average twenty-year-old is higher, not lower, than that of the average fifty-year-old.

A similar problem is that different preferences for present versus future consumption lead to measured differences in incomes for a given period. Consider two people who have the same earnings over their lifetimes. If one saves 20 percent of his income each year early in life, while the other saves only 10 percent, they will have quite different incomes when they reach middle age. Or, consider two high school graduates, one of whom goes to work while the other goes to college. The first will have a higher income early in life while the second will have a higher income later in life. Their incomes would be very unequal in any one year, but might be equal over their lifetimes.

The foregoing examples suggest but a few of the many reasons why measured differences in money incomes in a particular year are likely to overstate the degree of inequality. Of course, these factors can sometimes give the appearance of greater equality than actually exists: two people may have the same annual money income, but one of them works only two months of the year and the other works the full year. However, there is little doubt that the net effect is to overstate the degree of inequality. Even if this were not true, measured income inequalities give little or no guidance for determining who should be considered relatively affluent and who relatively poor for redistributive purposes.

Considering all of the factors that influence the distribution of income, it is understandable that we do not know how to ascertain the relative importance of each of them. Table 5-3 gives some information which suggests that money-income differences tend to exaggerate the degree of inequality. This table, like Table 2-2, is based on classifying families by money income according to whether they are in the lowest fifth, the second fifth, and so on. As can be seen, average family size increases with income. (This may seem surprising at first glance, but it is largely due to the fact that elderly

---

Table 5-3

FAMILY SIZE AND NUMBER OF EARNERS, BY PERCENTAGE DISTRIBUTION OF MONEY INCOME, 1973

Income Class	Average Family Size	Average Number of Earners	Percent of Family Members Who Are Earners
Lowest quintile	2.95	0.85	29
Second quintile	3.26	1.46	45
Third quintile	3.51	1.73	49
Fourth quintile	3.67	2.02	55
Highest quintile	3.80	2.26	59

Source: U.S. Bureau of the Census, *Current Population Reports*, series P-60, no. 97, "Money Income in 1973 of Families and Persons in the United States," (1975), Table 17.

families whose children have grown up and formed separate families are disproportionately represented in the lowest two quintiles.) Thus, even though there is more total income in the highest quintile, this income supports almost 30 percent more people than does income in the lowest quintile. If the Census Bureau's family income statistics were converted to a per capita basis the distribution would thus be less unequal.

The importance of leisure also varies markedly from quintile to quintile, as can be seen from the last two columns in Table 5-3. Only 29 percent of those in the lowest quintile are employed, while 59 percent of those in the highest quintile are employed. Thus, low-income families consume more leisure per family member than do higher-income families. In fact, according to Arnold Packer, differences in the number of earners per family is statistically the second most important source of inequality in family incomes, accounting for about one-third of measured inequality.[13] The most important source of inequality is different earnings per earner. Differences in property income are of negligible importance—at least when we consider inequality among quintiles.

Differences in money incomes are thus not very accurate gauges of differences in real incomes. The important implication of this finding is that redistribution from families with high money incomes to those with low money incomes can actually increase the degree of inequality in real income.

Even if we waive these kinds of difficulties, it is still not clear why equality in material circumstances should be considered desirable. Leland Yeager distinguishes between redistribution to help the very poor and redistribution aimed at chopping down very high incomes. Regarding leveling down high incomes, he observes:

> Why should it disturb us that some people are very wealthy? If we are unwilling to tolerate great superiorities in income and wealth, how do we feel about superiorities in talent, physical and mental strength and health, influence through family connections and personal friendships, ability and time to appreciate conversation and art and music and sports, amount of formal education, experience gained through travel, and so forth? People's circumstances can be different in innumerable ways. Why do redistributionists single out material inequality unless they think that money is—and should be—the prime measure of a man's capacity to enjoy life and of his worth to himself and other people, his social status, and his personal dignity? The reason cannot be that material inequality is the only kind susceptible of being leveled down.[14]

Making material equality the goal would be understandable if people were alike in all respects except material means. If people were identical in terms of age, family size and composition, health, status, intelligence, and other uncountable ways, then and only then would moving money from high- to low-income families seem an obviously desirable policy. When people are unavoidably different in many other respects, redistribution for the sake of income equality can only be described as materialistic. Of course, some may believe that government could, or should, take account of factors other than money income in determining the "just" distribution. But the power and the wisdom that government officials would have to possess in order to implement that vision strain the imagination. There are good reasons why a society that values freedom should restrict the discretionary power of government by requiring that taxes and transfers be based on a few objective characteristics, like money income and family size. Yet this means that government redistribution is, at best, a clumsy device to be used with circumspection.

Some people will regard these remarks as an attempt to defend obviously unacceptable degrees of inequality. It is easy to see how concern over whether equality is desirable and emphasis on the inadequacies of defining equality in terms of annual money income can be viewed as petty compared to the desperate needs of the poor. But it must be recognized that the importance of these considerations depends greatly on the amount of redistribution being contemplated. If we were discussing a moderate volume of redistribution to the bottom 10 or 15 percent of the population, to be financed by taxes on the upper 85 to 90 percent, the points raised in this section would be of quite minor significance. The importance of getting financial assistance to the very poor would overwhelm warnings that annual money income is not a perfect indicator of levels of well-being.

But that is emphatically not the situation in the United States today. At the present time, net transfers of at least $80 billion are already being made to the bottom one-fourth of the population. In all probability, at least a third of the population now receives net transfers from the other two-thirds. As stressed in the last section, from this point on any additional redistribution would increasingly shift money around within the middle-income classes. Of necessity, it would take place largely within the $5,000 to $15,000 income range (using Census Bureau measures) where more than half of all families reside. When the question involves massive redistribution that would occur largely in this range of incomes, doubts about the ethical justification for viewing a move towards equality in money incomes as desirable seem hardly misplaced.

The Political Process and Redistribution

Writing in 1962, Milton Friedman warned that the major disadvantage of an NIT stemmed from its political implications: [15]

> It establishes a system under which taxes are imposed on some to pay subsidies to others. And presumably, these others have a vote. There is always the danger that instead of being an arrangement under which the great majority tax themselves willingly to help an unfortunate minority, it will be converted into one under which a majority imposes taxes for its own benefit on an unwilling minority. Because this proposal makes the process so explicit, the danger is perhaps greater than with other measures.

This problem is not unique to the NIT, of course, but exists for any redistributive system of taxes and transfers. In fact, Friedman later changed his mind and contended that this danger was greater for existing programs than for the NIT.[16] That the net redistribution to the lowest quarter of the population tripled between 1966 and 1973, a period which saw a modest variant of the NIT rejected by the political process, tends to support this conclusion.

As long as the recipients of transfers vote, it is almost certain that the volume of resources transferred will be expanded beyond the level a majority of the taxpayers would want. Actually, this need not be regarded as unequivocally bad since it might be that if the taxpayers alone had the power to decide, they would redistribute too little. But more is involved here than the possibility that the political process will redistribute "too little" or "too much." The more important point is that the use of political power by potential recipients to augment their incomes is likely to be divisive. Redistribution unavoidably divides society into two groups, those who gain and those who bear the costs. Thus, taxpayers may decide on their own to make some redistribution to the poor, but if the political process transfers more than that amount, the interests of recipients and taxpayers will inevitably clash, and there will be no basis for an agreement acceptable to both sides. Whatever the outcome, the result will be an uneasy compromise with resentment on both sides.

Redistribution is one of the most important functions of government, but it is also potentially one of the most dangerous to the stability of a society. Increasingly, as people's relative standards of living are determined politically, antagonism is directed both at the system that produces the outcome and at those "other" selfish interests which are depriving each person of his "just share of the pie." There are signs that dissatisfactions of this type are growing: welfare militancy is a comparatively recent phenomenon, as is the taxpayer's revolt.

In part, dissatisfaction is due to an inability to understand the net effects of the present welfare system on the distribution of income. The incredible complexity of the welfare and tax systems can hardly be overemphasized. By selectively considering only some of the hundreds of government programs, it is possible to make almost any position sound plausible—that the system is pro-poor, pro-rich, pro-middle class, pro-black, pro-white, pro-the aged, and so on. Politicians, and others as well, are not above using this ploy. Given the nature of the present system, it is simply extraordinarily difficult to determine "the facts."

The lesson I draw from this is that it is crucial to have a system where people can easily get at least a rough understanding of how government affects the distribution of income. Distributional questions become all the harder to resolve when there is little agreement on what is already being done. If this conclusion is correct, then simplification of the welfare system should have a high priority on any reform agenda. The only way this can be accomplished is by replacing most existing programs with a negative income tax or with some other broad-based transfer program.

Attempts at piecemeal reform are hardly likely to bring about real improvement. Perhaps the best evidence of the dangers inherent in trying to tamper with an almost incomprehensible system is afforded by Nixon's Family Assistance Plan. As we have mentioned, the House of Representatives actually passed a version of this plan which would have imposed—unintentionally, to be sure—marginal tax rates above 100 percent on millions of people. That action illustrates dramatically how a misunderstanding of the present system, fostered by its complexity, can produce undesirable results. To repeat, it is not feasible to pile an NIT, or any other major program (such as some of the forms of national health insurance that have been proposed) on top of existing programs. It is to the credit of the Senate Finance Committee that it recognized FAP's defects and allowed the bill to die. Even so, Daniel Moynihan has stated that the real reason for the demise of the FAP was political, not substantive.[17]

Any attempt to substitute an NIT for the present system would encounter tough political resistance, because of the broad range of special interest groups that obtains substantial advantages under the current array of policies. One of these groups, usually not thought of as such, is strategically situated: the government employees who administer the current 168 federal programs and who have an understandably strong interest in their continuance. Their influence is disproportionate, not only because they provide most of the information used to guide policy decisions, but also because only they can claim "really" to understand how the policies operate. Friedrich Hayek's description of this new breed of experts is appropriate here:

> The new kind of expert . . . is an expert in a particular institutional setup. The organizations we have created in these fields have grown so complex that it takes more or less the whole of a person's time to master them. The institutional expert is not necessarily a person who knows all that is needed to enable him to judge the value of the institution, but frequently he is the only one who understands its organization fully and who therefore is indispensable. . . . But, almost invariably, this new kind of expert has one distinguishing characteristic: he is unhesitatingly in favor of the institutions on which he is expert. This is so not merely because only one who approves of the aims of the institution will have the interest and the patience to master the details, but even more because such an effort would hardly be worth the while of anybody else. . . .[18]

This group may well constitute the greatest obstacle to meaningful reform of the welfare system. According to Moynihan, the social welfare profession did everything in its power to block the FAP, even though that program would have replaced only a minor part of the existing system. It would be one thing if this opposition had been based on the proposal's substantive defects, but Moynihan's account suggests that it stemmed simply from a desire to preserve the present programs. Of the tactics of this group, he remarks: "They are not to be judged more greedy than the average interest group, but neither did they show themselves to be other than an interest group, one representing middle-class professional interests at that." [19]

A simple welfare system is necessary if the voters and the Congress are to understand it well enough to make informed judgments on distributional matters. When the system cannot easily be understood, effective control will gravitate to the "experts," that is, the bureaucracy.

Another of the undesirable political side effects of relying on innumerable programs to redistribute income is that attention is distracted from other issues. Legislators have to try to keep informed on hundreds of programs and to make frequent alterations in these policies. The time of legislators is a very scarce resource, and the more time devoted to fine-tuning the distribution of income, the less is available for other issues like foreign policy, inflation, and environmental matters. It may be that poor performance in these other areas is a major cost of preoccupation with distributional programs.

Redistribution is an important government function, but our current handling of it leaves much to be desired. Indeed, decisions on the appropriate method and level of redistribution may be of the kind that should be insulated, to some degree, from the pressures of day-to-day politics. One way of accomplishing this would be a constitutional amendment specifying the method and maximum level of federal redistribution. Although this approach involves many practical problems, the advantages of removing the sensitive distributional issue from the normal political arena might be great enough to justify serious consideration of some reform of this type.

CHAPTER VI

CONCLUDING REMARKS

In this study I have attempted to give an objective overview of the economic aspects of redistributive policies. But complete objectivity is a will o' the wisp, and my personal views have undoubtedly intruded on the analysis to some degree—both through the selection of topics to be covered and in other, less obvious ways. For that reason, I wish to make explicit my own views on some of the issues discussed.

Until recently, I usually summarized my views about redistribution with two statements: first, that governments engage in too much redistribution and, second, that governments do not redistribute enough to the poorest families. It should be noted that these propositions are not inconsistent since a large share of the resources redistributed are simply shifted around in the middle-income classes.

The first proposition still appears basically sound. Participants in the political process are preoccupied with using government power to dispense favors to special groups. But this is done for so many groups that the result is what has been aptly called "criss-crossing" redistribution: group A pays taxes that finance a transfer to group B, but group B pays taxes that finance a transfer to group A. There is an immense amount of redistribution of this type: recall that more than half of all social welfare expenditures do *not* benefit the poorest quarter of the population. It is not clear who actually benefits on balance from all this redistribution. What is clear is that sizeable distortions have been introduced into the system by the tax, expenditure, and regulatory policies used to carry out these transfers.

Whereas the first proposition still seems defensible to me, the second proposition does not. The volume of redistribution to the low-income population is much greater than I had thought possible. A year ago I would have guessed that the net transfer to the lowest quartile was not more than $40 billion, but the evidence produced in this study suggests that the correct figure is about twice this. My initial, erroneous belief was based on an inability to reconcile the small decline in the official poverty population with transfers as immense as $80 billion. Of course, my error was in not recognizing how important in-kind transfers have become in recent years.

If this estimate of the net transfer to the lowest quartile is approximately correct, then it follows from the analysis in Chapter 5 that additional redistribution to the low-income population will necessitate extremely high marginal tax rates on all families. The additional distortions produced by still higher tax rates would be quite sizeable, and I question whether the tenuous advantages of a still more equal distribution of income are worth this cost. Unless we are willing to impose effective marginal tax rates in excess of 50 percent, there is little scope for increasing the share of the national product being transferred to the low-income population. Indeed, I believe it is time to consider the possibility that we may already have gone too far in mobilizing the power of the state to produce a more equal distribution of income.

For many years one of the prime concerns of reformers has been the "adequacy" of benefit levels in the welfare system. This has generally motivated an effort to redistribute more and more resources to the poor, an effort that has been eminently successful in recent years. Today, with a vastly larger and more complex welfare system, reform is more urgent than ever. What is needed, however, is not the addition of some new program, or the expansion of existing ones, but a major overhaul designed to streamline and simplify the entire system. The major inequities and distortions of the existing system are the predictable and unavoidable outcomes of an effort to coordinate hundreds of policies, and nothing short of elimination of most of these policies in favor of a uniform broad-based cash transfer program is likely to improve matters significantly.

NOTES

NOTES TO CHAPTER II

[1] For the expenditure figures, see A. M. Skolnik and S. R. Dales, "Social Welfare Expenditures," *Social Security Bulletin*, vol. 37, no. 1 (January 1974), pp. 3-68; for numbers of poor persons, see U.S. Bureau of the Census, "Characteristics of the Low-Income Population, 1973," *Current Population Reports*, series P-60, no. 98 (1975), Table 1.

[2] For example, John F. Due and Ann F. Friedlander assert: "In general the share of national income accruing to the poorest fifth of the population has remained distressingly constant during the past 50-60 years." John F. Due and Ann F. Friedlander, *Government Finance: Economics of the Public Sector* (Homewood, Ill.: Richard D. Irwin, Inc., 1973), p. 133. This conclusion is frequently reached by those who interpret the Census Bureau's estimates of the percentage distribution of money income (see Table 2-2) as an accurate measure of relative standards of living. As we shall see, these frequently cited figures have become increasingly unreliable as measures of relative living standards.

[3] The Bureau of the Census also publishes a distribution for unrelated individuals and for families plus unrelated individuals. Since unrelated individuals only comprise 8 percent of the population, I have ignored these other distributions.

Although the distribution in Table 2-1 is widely referred to as a before-tax distribution, it reflects the impact of indirect taxes (like corporate income taxes and excise taxes). More precisely, it is a distribution before direct taxes like income and payroll taxes. Since direct taxes are progressive, the after-tax distribution of income is more equal than the Census Bureau's distribution of money income.

[4] For a discussion of the definition of income used, see U.S. Bureau of the Census, "Money Income in 1972 of Families and Persons in the United States," *Current Population Reports*, series P-60, no. 90 (1973), pp. 10-11.

[5] Cash transfers from government tend to be underreported. Social security payments are reported at about 89 percent of their actual amount and public assistance payments at about 75 percent. (U.S. Bureau of the Census, "Characteristics of the Low-Income Population: 1973," *Current Population Reports*, series P-60, no. 98, p. 159).

[6] It might be thought that government transfers played a large role in increasing the low money incomes, but we will see that they played a relatively minor role compared to economic growth.

[7] Mollie Orshansky, "Counting the Poor: Another Look at the Poverty Profile," *Social Security Bulletin*, vol. 28 (January 1965), pp. 3-13.

[8] Rose Friedman persuasively argues that the criterion used to define poverty, that is, nutritional adequacy, was misused and this misuse led to an estimate of the number of poor persons that was much too large. See Rose D. Friedman, *Poverty: Definition and Perspective* (Washington, D. C.: American Enterprise Institute, 1965).

[9] This is just a rough guess since there are no detailed estimates of the distribution of world income. However, it is probably conservative: see United Nations, *Statistical Yearbook 1973* (New York, 1974), Table 182, p. 590, which

lists only a handful of countries with per capita incomes as high as one-fourth the level of the United States.

[10] See Table 2-7.

[11] These figures are given in Barry M. Blechman, Edward M. Gramlich, and Robert W. Hartman, *Setting National Priorities: The 1975 Budget* (Washington, D. C.: The Brookings Institution, 1974), p. 170. The figures are based on a study by Michael C. Barth, George J. Carcagno, and John L. Palmer that I have not seen.

[12] Joseph A. Pechman and Benjamin A. Okner give estimates for the under-$3,000 income class (1966). The estimates range from 18 to 24 percent for seven sets of incidence assumptions and reach 28 percent for an extreme incidence assumption. See Pechman and Okner, *Who Bears the Tax Burden?* (Washington, D. C.: The Brookings Institution, 1974), p. 49.

[13] Benjamin A. Okner, "Transfer Payments: Their Distribution and Role in Reducing Poverty," in *Redistribution to the Rich and the Poor*, ed. Kenneth E. Boulding and Martin Pfaff (Belmont, California: Wadsworth Publishing Company, 1972), pp. 62-76.

[14] Robert J. Lampman, "How Much Does the American System of Transfers Benefit the Poor?" in *Economic Progress and Social Welfare*, ed. L. H. Goodman, 93rd Annual Forum, National Conference on Social Welfare (New York: Columbia University Press, 1966), pp. 125-157.

[15] I did not include the year 1947 since the particular percentages assumed for the components of social welfare expenditures are likely to be more inaccurate that far into the past.

[16] For example, see Okner, *Redistribution to the Rich and the Poor*, p. 65, who gives the 6 percent figure. This is close to the 5.8 percent figure derived by Richard A. Musgrave and Peggy B. Musgrave, *Public Finance in Theory and Practice* (New York: McGraw-Hill Book Company, 1973), p. 656.

Actually it is not strictly correct to subtract all taxes if we are concerned with how many will have incomes above their poverty lines, since the poverty lines are based on incomes before payment of *some* of these taxes.

[17] Education "benefits" here refers to the resource cost of education. The $11.8 billion figure for 1973 does not mean that this was the value actually placed on these resources by the low-income population.

[18] Okner, *Redistribution to the Rich and the Poor*, p. 65, gives a figure of $22.7 billion for 1966. If the pretransfer income of the lowest quartile grew by the same rate as GNP, it would have reached $38.6 billion in 1973. I assume a lower rate of growth bringing the figure to $30 billion, so the final estimate may be conservative.

[19] These figures are based on those officially defined as poor in 1972; see U.S. Bureau of the Census, "Characteristics of the Low-Income Population, 1972," *Current Population Reports*, series P-60, no. 91 (1973), Table 2. It is probable that the number of unrelated individuals is an even smaller fraction of the entire lowest quartile since this group constitutes only 8 percent of the entire population.

[20] See Table 2-9 below.

[21] See Blechman, Gramlich, and Hartman, *Setting National Priorities*, p. 168. The federal programs included in this tabulation, however, include only about 85 percent of all federal social welfare programs.

[22] The "Other" category includes community action, model cities, social services, child care, and other programs. All of the specific programs identified by HEW in this category are apparently in-kind programs.

[23] This figure can be calculated from Tables 5 and 38, U.S. Bureau of the Census, "Characteristics of the Low-Income Population: 1973," *Current Population Reports*, series P-60, no. 98.

[24] This is a rough estimate based on a detailed breakdown of the poor by earnings class for 1968 given by Bradley R. Schiller, *The Economics of Poverty and Discrimination* (Englewood Cliffs, N. J.: Prentice-Hall, Inc., 1973), pp. 54-55.

[25] This is a rough estimate arrived at in the following way: Of $122.3 billion in federal social welfare expenditures in 1973, $26.2 billion, or 21.4 percent of the total, benefited the poor. In calculating the $7.4 billion figure, I assumed that 21.4 percent of total state and local social welfare expenditures (excluding education) of $34.6 billion also accrued to the poor.

[26] It should be noted that taxes paid by the poor have not been subtracted in computing this estimate. This is the correct procedure since the poverty lines are in terms of income before payment of direct taxes.

[27] The total money income of the poor can be calculated directly from information in U.S. Bureau of the Census, "Characteristics of the Low-Income Population: 1973," Table 38, by multiplying the mean income for poor families and unrelated individuals by their respective numbers. This yields a figure of $18.5 billion. However, my estimate of $20.8 billion is probably more accurate since respondents to the Current Population Survey typically underreport money income by about 10 percent on average. Money transfers, which form a large part of the total money income of the poor, are typically underreported by more than 10 percent. See U.S. Bureau of the Census, "Money Income in 1972 of Families and Persons in the United States," *Current Population Reports*, series P-60, no. 90 (1973), pp. 24-25.

[28] These figures are not exactly comparable since the $1,248 figure is a net transfer that makes allowance for all taxes paid whereas the $1,461 figure makes no allowance for direct taxes. I have seen no estimates of direct taxes paid by the poor so I have not attempted to make any adjustment for this.

[29] It is certainly the case that substantial transfers are received by those in the lowest quartile who are not officially poor. Recall that 9 percent of all U.S. families were made nonpoor by receiving transfers, and most of these would still be in the lowest quartile.

[30] There are no reliable estimates of the distribution of in-kind transfers by income class, so this is a very rough estimate. It is based on the assumption of total in-kind transfers of $35 billion in 1973, with $22 billion accruing to the lowest quintile of families. Although admittedly imprecise, this estimate is probably conservative. Recall that in-kind transfers to the poor by the federal government alone amounted to $15.1 billion in 1973 (see Table 2-9) and that the poor were only about 11 percent of the population in that year.

[31] This will be shown in the discussion of some of the individual programs in the next chapter.

[32] The age distribution in the lowest quintile changed over this period. The proportion of families with a head over sixty-five years of age increased from 32.0 to 34.0 percent, and the proportion of families with heads between fourteen and twenty-four years increased from 6.3 to 12.9 percent. These changes are certainly part of the explanation for the figures in Table 2-10.

[33] Other analysts have found a decrease in income from work on the part of recipients of transfers. With respect to the food stamp program, David H. Greenberg and Marvin Kosters have concluded that the decrease is "roughly equal to the subsidy so that the two cancel out and there is no net gain in income. This suggests that offering food stamps [to the working poor] results in no net gain, except in increased leisure for the participants." (Greenberg and Kosters, "Income Guarantees and the Working Poor: The Effect of Income-Maintenance Programs on the Hours of Work of Male Family Heads," in G. G. Cain and H. W. Watts, eds. *Income Maintenance and Labor Supply* (Chicago: Rand McNally Publishing Co., 1973), p. 69.

[34] Gordon Tullock, "The Charity of the Uncharitable," *Western Economic Journal*, vol. 9 (December 1971), p. 379.

[35] Gordon Tullock, "More on the Welfare Cost of Transfers," *Kyklos*, vol. 2 (1974).

[36] Joseph Pechman, "The Rich, the Poor, and the Taxes They Pay," *Public Interest*, vol. 17 (Fall 1969), p. 43.

37 Philip M. Stern, *The Rape of the American Taxpayer* (New York: Random House, 1973). Roger Freeman provides a more balanced view of the loopholes question in *Tax Loopholes*, AEI-Hoover Policy Study (Washington, D. C.: American Enterprise Institute, 1973).

NOTES TO CHAPTER III

1 There is a small companion program to AFDC that covers some families headed by males: AFDC-UF (Unemployed Father). This program operated in only about half the states in 1971, and coverage was very limited. It will be ignored in our discussion.

2 These figures are from Tables 7-1 and 7-3 in Barry M. Blechman, Edward M. Gramlich, and Robert W. Hartman, *Setting National Priorties: The 1975 Budget*, pp. 167, 170.

3 Bradley R. Schiller, *The Economics of Poverty and Discrimination*, p. 151.

4 Further evidence that the low labor force participation among the aged is the result of voluntary choice is given by Lowell E. Gallaway, *Poverty in America* (Columbus, Ohio: Grid, Inc., 1973), pp. 125-127.

5 U.S. Congress, Joint Economic Committee, Subcommittee on Fiscal Policy, *Studies in Public Welfare*, Paper No. 14, 93rd Congress, 2nd session, 1974, p. 3. This study on "Public Welfare and Work Incentives: Theory and Practice," is by Vee Burke and Alair A. Townsend.

6 Martin Feldstein, "Unemployment Compensation: Adverse Incentives and Distributional Anomalies," *National Tax Journal*, vol. 27 (June 1974), pp. 231-244.

7 U.S. Congress, Joint Economic Committee, Subcommittee on Fiscal Policy, *Studies on Public Welfare*, Paper No. 12, Part I, 93rd Congress, 1st session, November 1973. Study on "The Impact of Welfare Payment Levels on Family Stability," by Marjorie Honig, pp. 51, 38.

8 Arlene Holen and Stanley A. Horowitz, "The Effect of Unemployment Insurance and Eligibility Enforcement on Unemployment," *The Journal of Law and Economics*, vol. 17 (October 1974), pp. 403-431.

9 For a recent thorough analysis of the food stamp program, see Kenneth W. Clarkson, *Food Stamps and Nutrition* (Washington, D. C.: American Enterprise Institute, 1975).

10 Strictly speaking, eligibility requirements are specified in terms of monthly income. I have translated the figures to their annual equivalents in order to facilitate comparison with the NIT.

11 In theory, because of the restriction on food consumption, the food stamp program may not have exactly the same effect on work effort as an $1,800-30% NIT: work effort may fall by more or less than under the NIT. (See Barry L. Friedman and Leonard J. Hausman, "Income Conditioning in a System of Transfer Programs," *American Economic Review*, vol. 64 [May 1974], pp. 175-180.) However, when in-kind transfers are made for several important goods in the consumer's budget any differential effects on work effort are likely to be slight.

12 Clarkson, *Food Stamps and Nutrition*, p. 42.

13 Richard F. Muth, *Public Housing: An Economic Evaluation* (Washington, D. C.: American Enterprise Institute, 1973), p. 2.

14 John Kraft (Federal Energy Administration) and Edgar O. Olsen (University of Virginia), "An Evaluation of Public Housing," unpublished manuscript, July 1973.

15 Sam Peltzman has recently emphasized this possibility with regard to higher education subsidies. See Peltzman, "The Effect of Government Subsidies-in-Kind on Private Expenditures: The Case of Higher Education," *Journal of Political Economy*, vol. 81 (January/February 1973), pp. 1-27.

[16] John Kraft and Edgar O. Olsen, "The Distribution of Benefits from Public Housing," in *The Distribution of Economic Well-Being*, vol. 61 of *Studies in Income and Wealth* (New York: National Bureau of Economic Research, forthcoming).

[17] *U.S. News & World Report*, vol. 77 (July 22, 1974), p. 33, states that 15 million are receiving aid out of 37-50 million eligible. Participation is highest in the low-income groups where the subsidies are largest. That many who are eligible are not yet receiving benefits probably means that the program will continue to grow even if benefit levels are not increased.

[18] Kraft and Olsen, "An Evaluation of Public Housing," p. 42.

[19] Clarkson, *Food Stamps and Nutrition*, p. 50.

[20] I have examined the externality argument for in-kind transfers more carefully in "The Externality Argument for In-Kind Transfers: Some Critical Remarks," *Kyklos* (forthcoming).

[21] Bernard Lander, *Towards an Understanding of Juvenile Delinquency*, (New York: Columbia University Press, 1954).

[22] Muth, *Public Housing*, pp. 31-41, discusses the scant evidence that exists.

[23] I have developed the following argument more rigorously in "The Diagrammatic Analysis of Multiple Consumption Externalities," *American Economic Review*, vol. 64 (September 1974), pp. 707-714.

[24] This assumes that the marginal and average propensities to consume these goods are equal. Actually, the marginal propensity is probably slightly below the average propensity, but even so it is a safe bet that two-thirds of a cash transfer would be spent on housing, food, and medical care by most low-income families.

[25] Clarkson, *Food Stamps and Nutrition*, p. 30, and Kraft and Olsen, "An Evaluation of Public Housing," p. 37.

[26] Report of the President's Commission on Income Maintenance Programs, *Poverty Amid Plenty: The American Paradox* (Washington, D. C.: U.S. Government Printing Office, 1969), p. 62.

[27] Harrison G. Wehner, Jr., *Sections 235 and 236: An Economic Evaluation of HUD's Principal Housing Subsidy Programs* (Washington, D. C.: American Enterprise Institute, 1973), pp. 14-15.

[28] For two helpful surveys of manpower and training studies, see U.S. Congress, Joint Economic Committee, Subcommittee on Fiscal Policy, *Studies in Public Welfare*, Paper No. 3, 92nd Congress, 2nd session, 1972, a study on "The Effectiveness of Manpower Training Programs: A Review of Research on the Impact on the Poor" by Jon H. Goldstein; and Steve L. Barsby, *Cost-Benefit Analysis and Manpower Programs* (Lexington: D. C. Heath and Company, 1972).

[29] This study is discussed in Goldstein, *Studies in Public Welfare*, p. 6.

[30] In Table 1, Goldstein, *Studies in Public Welfare*, indicates that the total first time enrollments over the 1963-71 period were 6.1 million. In the Appendix to Burke and Townsend, *Studies in Public Welfare*, figures show that about 2.5 million were enrolled in 1973. I do not have estimates for 1972, but would guess from total expenditure figures that enrollments were well in excess of the 1.4 million necessary to bring the 1963-73 total to 10 million.

[31] See Gallaway, *Poverty in America*.

[32] Ibid., pp. 148-149.

[33] The most thorough study on tax incidence is the recent one by Joseph A. Pechman and Benjamin A. Okner, *Who Bears the Tax Burden?* (Washington, D. C., The Brookings Institution, 1974). They develop eight separate sets of estimates, based on alternative assumptions about tax incidence. For the below $3,000 class the estimates range from 18 to 28 percent, somewhat lower than in most other studies.

[34] For example, see Pechman, "The Rich, the Poor, and the Taxes They Pay," *Public Interest*, no. 17 (Fall 1969), pp. 21-43.

[35] This analysis does not imply what is the appropriate share of the cost for poor families, or other families, to bear. I am simply emphasizing the

importance of their bearing some positive share of the costs. For an important discussion of tax institutions as cost-sharing devices in a democracy, see James M. Buchanan, *Public Finance in the Democratic Process* (Chapel Hill: University of North Carolina Press, 1967).

[36] For a useful survey of the evidence on this point see John M. Peterson and Charles T. Stewart, Jr., *Employment Effects of Minimum Wage Rates* (Washington, D. C.: American Enterprise Institute, 1969).

[37] This example is taken from Burke and Townsend, *Studies in Public Welfare*, pp. 28-29.

[38] U.S. Congress, Joint Economic Committee, Subcommittee on Fiscal Policy, *Studies in Public Welfare*, Paper No. 1, 92nd Congress, 2nd session, 1972. Study on "Public Income Transfer Programs: The Incidence of Multiple Benefits and the Issues Raised by Their Receipt," by James R. Storey, p. 12.

[39] Ibid., p. 33.

[40] Henry J. Aaron, *Why Is Welfare So Hard to Reform?* (Washington, D. C.: The Brookings Institution, 1973), gives numerous examples of how the interrelationships among transfer programs can work to destroy incentives.

[41] Although nominally levied on both employers and employees, it is widely agreed among economists that employees bear the burden of both parts. For a recent examination of the theory and evidence, see John A. Brittain, *The Payroll Tax for Social Security* (Washington, D. C.: The Brookings Institution, 1972).

[42] The effective marginal tax rate can not always be calculated simply by adding the rates in the separate programs because the income bases for calculating the tax or transfer may vary from one program to another. I have ignored this complication in the text.

[43] Henry J. Aaron, *Why Is Welfare So Hard to Reform?* pp. 32-38. This helpful study emphasizes the "cumulative tax rate" problem of multiple programs.

[44] U.S. Congress, Senate, Committee on Finance, *Hearings on Establishing Priorities among Programs Aiding the Poor*, 92nd Congress, 2nd session, February 1972.

[45] As reported in Robert I. Lerman and Alair A. Townsend, "Conflicting Objectives in Income Maintenance Programs," *American Economic Review*, vol. 64 (May 1974), p. 209.

[46] Blechman, Gramlich, and Hartman, *Setting National Priorities*, p. 185.

NOTES TO CHAPTER IV

[1] These are very rough estimates.

[2] See Ralph D. Husby, "Work Incentives and the Cost Effectiveness of Income Maintenance Programs," *Quarterly Review of Economics and Business*, vol. 13 (Spring 1973), pp. 7-13. Husby gives more precise estimates of the effect of reductions in earnings on cost than the figures I mention.

[3] Arnold Harberger shows that under plausible conditions an income tax will produce a smaller distortion than an equal-yield excise tax. The same argument can be applied to a negative income tax compared with excise subsidies (or other forms of in-kind transfers). See Arnold C. Harberger, "Taxation, Resource Allocation, and Welfare," in *The Role of Direct and Indirect Taxes in the Federal Revenue System* (Princeton: Princeton University Press for the National Bureau of Economic Research and the Brookings Institution, 1964), pp. 25-70.

[4] There are three other income-maintenance experiments in addition to this one, but the results are available only for the New Jersey-Pennsylvania experiment.

[5] U.S. Congress, Joint Economic Committee, Subcommittee on Fiscal Policy, *Studies in Public Welfare*, Paper No. 13, 93rd Congress, 2nd session, February 1974, pp. 1-32. This study on "Income Transfer Programs and Work Effort: A Review" by Irwin Garfinkel is a very helpful review of the available evidence. See also Vee Burke and Alair A. Townsend, *Studies in Public Welfare.*

[6] Albert Rees surveys the experimental findings in "An Overview of the Labor-Supply Results," *The Journal of Human Resources*, vol. 9 (Spring 1974), pp. 158-180. This entire issue of *The Journal of Human Resources* is devoted to discussions of the results of the New Jersey experiment.

[7] The experiment actually tried several alternative NIT plans. The 6 and 15 percent figures are averages for all the plans used.

[8] I have discussed this point in "Incentive and Disincentive Experimentation for Income Maintenance Policy Purposes: Note," *American Economic Review*, vol. 61 (September 1971), pp. 709-712.

[9] See Richard Goode, *The Individual Income Tax* (Washington, D. C.: The Brookings Institution, 1964).

[10] This is the type of plan recommended by the President's Commission on Income Maintenance Programs; see Report of the President's Commission on Income Maintenance Programs, *Poverty Amid Plenty: The American Paradox*, pp. 57-63.

[11] The Tax Reduction Act of 1975 (P.L. 94-12) increased the low-income allowance to $1,600. Since the increase is scheduled to expire at the end of 1975, it is not reflected in the figures used in this study.

[12] Milton Friedman, "The Case for the Negative Income Tax," in *Republican Papers*, ed. Melvin Laird (New York: Doubleday and Company, Inc., 1968), pp. 202-220.

[13] Jonathan R. Kesselman, "Labor-Supply Effects of Income, Income-Work, and Wage Subsidies," *The Journal of Human Resources*, vol. 4 (Summer 1969), pp. 275-292; "Conditional Subsidies in Income Maintenance," *Western Economic Journal*, vol. 9 (March 1971), pp. 1-20; "A Comprehensive Approach to Income Maintenance: SWIFT," *Journal of Public Economics*, vol. 2 (February 1973), pp. 59-88; Richard Zeckhauser, "Optimal Mechanisms for Income Transfers," *American Economic Review*, vol. 61 (June 1971), pp. 324-334; Richard Zeckhauser and Peter Schuck, "An Alternative to the Nixon Income Maintenance Plan," *Public Interest*, vol. 19 (Spring 1970), pp. 120-130; Edgar K. Browning, "Alternative Programs for Income Redistribution: The NIT and the NWT," *American Economic Review*, vol. 63 (March 1973), pp. 38-49.

[14] Belton M. Fleisher, *Labor Economics: Theory and Evidence* (Englewood Cliffs, N. J.: Prentice-Hall, Inc., 1970), Chapter 3.

[15] See Browning, "Alternative Programs for Income Redistribution," pp. 38-49.

[16] See U.S. Congress, Joint Economic Committee, *The Economics of Federal Subsidy Programs, Higher Education and Manpower Subsidies*, Part 4, 92nd Congress, 2nd session, 1972, pp. 497-540. A study on "Universal Wage-Rate Subsidy: Benefits and Effects," by Michael C. Barth, emphasizes the difficulty of targeting benefits on the poor.

[17] Milton Friedman, "Welfare: Back to the Drawing Board," reprinted from *Newsweek* in Friedman, *An Economist's Protest* (Glen Ridge, New Jersey: Thomas Horton and Co., 1972), pp. 136-138.

[18] Ibid., p. 137.

NOTES TO CHAPTER V

[1] Harold Hochman and James Rodgers have elaborated on this point in "Pareto Optimal Redistribution," *American Economic Review*, vol. 59 (September 1969), pp. 542-557. For a discussion of related topics, see William

Breit, "Income Redistribution and Efficiency Norms," in *Redistribution Through Public Choice*, ed. H. M. Hochman and G. E. Peterson (New York: Columbia University Press, 1974), pp. 3-21.

[2] Lester Thurow, "Toward a Definition of Economic Justice," *Public Interest*, no. 31 (Spring 1973), p. 75.

[3] Report of the President's Commission on Income Maintenance Programs, *Poverty Amid Plenty: The American Paradox*, p. 61.

[4] Daniel P. Moynihan, *The Politics of a Guaranteed Income* (New York: Vintage Books, 1973), p. 344.

[5] See J. E. Meade, "Poverty in the Welfare State," *Oxford Economic Papers*, vol. 24 (November 1972), pp. 289-326, for an analysis that uses the approach adopted in the next several paragraphs.

[6] How much marginal tax rates must rise does depend to a degree on the type of demogrant used and the tax base employed to finance the outlays. The 5 percentage point figure given in the text is based on calculations using figures from Benjamin A. Okner's "The Role of Demogrants as an Income Maintenance Alternative" (discussed later in this chapter.) If it were possible to use NNP itself as a tax base, however, my calculations suggest that marginal tax rates might have to rise by as little as four percentage points in redistributing 1 percent of NNP for certain demogrant plans. However, it is not feasible to use a tax base that inclusive so the five percentage point figure is probably a more realistic estimate.

[7] Of course, the income effect of a higher average tax rate encourages more work effort. However, for redistributive programs, marginal tax rates will rise by much more than average tax rates, suggesting that the substitution effect will tend to be much more important than the income effect.

[8] The formula for estimating the welfare loss of a tax or transfer based on labor income is $(\frac{1}{2})em^2wL$, where e is the elasticity of labor supply (expressing the substitution effect alone), m is the marginal tax rate, w is the market wage rate, and L is the quantity of labor. See Arnold C. Harberger, "Taxation, Resource Allocation, and Welfare."

[9] While AGI excludes some items, like unrealized capital gains, that many feel ought to be subject to tax, these items are not large enough to materially affect the conclusions drawn in this paragraph.

[10] The figures on total AGI are from Roger Freeman, *Tax Loopholes*, p. 32.

[11] U.S. Congress, Joint Economic Committee, Subcommittee on Fiscal Policy, *Studies in Public Welfare*, Paper No. 9, 93rd Congress, 1st session, 1973. A study on "The Role of Demogrants as an Income Maintenance Alternative," by Benjamin A. Okner.

[12] These figures are based on Okner, Table 5 which shows these sums redistributed to the under-$3,000 income class, and Table 4, which shows that 26.8 percent of all families were in this class.

[13] U.S. Congress, Joint Economic Committee, Subcommittee on Fiscal Policy, *Studies in Public Welfare*, Paper No. 9, 93rd Congress, 1st session, 1973. A study on "Categorical Public Employment Guarantees: A Proposed Solution to the Poverty Problem," by Arnold C. Packer.

[14] Leland B. Yeager, "Can a Liberal Be an Equalitarian?" in *Toward Liberty*, F. A. von Hayek, Henry Hazlitt, Leonard E. Read, Gustavo R. Velasco, and F. A. Harper (Sponsoring Committee), vol. 2 (Menlo Park: Institute for Humane Studies, Inc., 1971), p. 433.

[15] Milton Friedman, *Capitalism and Freedom* (Chicago: University of Chicago Press, 1962), p. 194.

[16] Milton Friedman, "The Case for the Negative Income Tax," in *Republican Papers*, ed. Melvin Laird (New York: Doubleday and Company, Inc., 1968), pp. 202-220.

[17] See Moynihan, *Politics of a Guaranteed Income*. In reviewing Moynihan's book, Leonard J. Hausman argues that there were important substantive objections to FAP, and I think he is surely correct in this. See Hausman, "The Politics of a Guaranteed Income: The Nixon Administration and the Family Assistance Plan—A Review Article," *The Journal of Human Resources*, vol. 8 (Fall 1973), pp. 411-421.

[18] F. A. Hayek, *The Constitution of Liberty* (Chicago: University of Chicago Press, 1960), pp. 290-291.

[19] Moynihan, *Politics of a Guaranteed Income*, p. 321.

Book design: Pat Taylor